Aziz Bagh
The Heritage of Culture

By
Zaheer Ahmed

Other Books by the Author :

Dr. Zakir Hussain
One Solution
Ten Commandments
(A comparative Study)
One Religion
One Religion 101

Author's Next Publication:

Aziz Jung Heritage Genealogy Tree

This publication will include the Aziz Jung family tree which will include more than 550 names of the Aziz Jung descendents and their spouses.

Aziz Bagh
The Heritage of Culture

www.azizbagh.com

110 years of Aziz Bagh History, 1430 years of family trace.
This is our family story, this is our family elegance.

By
Zaheer Ahmed

First published 2009

Zaheer U. Ahmed
1720 Mundelein Road
Naperville, IL 60565-6785
USA

azizbagh@netnavigate.com

Authentication reviewed by:
Dr. Hasanuddin Ahmed
Ahmed Abdul Aziz
Razia Siddiqui

Editors:
Mansoor Khan
Hana Ahmed-Khan
Saba Ahmed

Statistics:
310 Pictures
188 pages
33,248 words

Printed in the USA

This book may be ordered from:
https://www.createspace.com/3377781

Disclaimer:

The Author informed all Aziz Bagh family members about this book in a timely manner. This book is an effort to recognize the individuals with their names only. Individual biographies and pictures are not the scope of this book, but some additional pictures and individual details are added due to individual requests. The author's intention is not to publish individual biographies. Author's knowledge is limited and as good as his resources. Any pictures or individual details missing are due the fact that these individuals did not provide the author with any pictures or details about them at the time of final publishing.

Dedicated
To my children
Mansoor, Hana, Sameer, Saba,
and the entire Aziz Bagh Family

Aziz Bagh picnic 2002 in Chicago

Aziz Bagh by day and night.

Contents

Front exit of Aziz Bagh.

Aziz Bagh surrounded by breath-taking landscaping.

Acknowledgements

Sincere thanks are due to the following for their patience, precious time, observations and valuable suggestions. Whether they realized it or not, they had a most profound influence on me.

Anees Hasanuddin Ahmed
Dr. Hasanuddin Ahmed
Shamsuddin Ahmed
Farzana Ahmed
Razia Ahmed
Ahmed Abdul Aziz
Razia Siddiqui

Pictures Courtesy:
Ali Ahmed
Anees Ahmed
Anees H. Ahmed
Hasanuddin Ahmed
Nasreen Ahmed
Zaheer Ahmed
Yawar Baig
Syed Omar Hussaini
Faraaz Kamran
Reema Kamran
Razia Siddiqui
Mohammed Zafarullah

Contributions to the book:
Anees Ahmed
Ruqhia Ali
Dr. Hamid Husain
Syed Asghar Hussaini
Syeda Zainab Hussaini
Zarina Qadeer
Yawar Baig
Mohammed Mohiuddin (Nasir)
Shirlee Mohiuddin
Aziz Qureshi
Mohammed Rahmathullah
Mohammed Azher Siddiqui
Mohammed Hakimuddin (Zakir) Siddiqui
Sabeen Siddiqui
Zaheer Siddiqui
Azra Waheed
Mohammed Zafarullah

Drawings:
Aziz Ahmed
Erum Ahmed

Pigeons at Aziz Bagh.

Preface

By Dr. Hasanuddin Ahmed

I am extremely happy that my son Zaheer is keeping up the noble family traditions. He could find time, in spite of his busy schedule, in the United States, to delve deep into his roots. He has prepared a pictorial monograph on Aziz Bagh, the name of his ancestral house in Hyderabad, India.

Zaheer asked me to go through the manuscript and to suggest any change or alteration. This I was not willing to do, as I thought I should not intrude into the flow of a young mind.

Zaheer then asked me to write a preface. I conceded. The difficulty and delicacy was that the expression of even facts will appear as boastfulness and egotistical. Whereas my attitude is:

Hum aib ke manind chhupate hain hunar aaj.

(Translation: These days our attitude is to conceal virtue as the vice is concealed)

At the same time, I felt the facts should be allowed to see the light of the day, not as glorification of a family or individuals but merely as a process of Cultural History.

To overcome the difficulty, I decided that 'Aziz Bagh' should be personified and allowed to tell all about itself, its founder and about those who lived or are living in it. Then only, I thought, there would be substance and force in what I wanted to say. The preface will then have some significance rather than remaining a mere formality. This will be an apt introduction to the subject dealt with in the book.

Let us then see what Aziz Bagh has to say,

I am Aziz Bagh.

One of the two houses given in the prestigious illustrated book 'Indian Style' by Suzanne Slasin and Stafford Cliff is me. In it, with the caption 'Artistic Centre' I am introduced as follows: "Built in 1899 in the suburbs of Hyderabad, the house always been a center for writers and artists".

The State Chapter of Indian National Trust for Cultural Heritage (INTACH) identified me as a Best Maintained Heritage Building and offered the present occupant the Heritage Award on 27th July 1997. While receiving the Award, the following couplet came to my mind extempore:

"Pahchani qadar aaj, taghaful to dekhiye
Sow saal pure hone ko do saal rah gaye"

(Translation: Look at their indifference! They have realized my value today when two years are left to its centenary)

My material, part of which is composed of bricks and mortar, is no doubt property of a joint family. As principles, character, and noble ideologies were also used as ingredients along with bricks and mortar, I represent a Culture. My history is part of our heritage. I am not only the name of a few buildings and a beautiful garden, but I am an institution by myself which has developed a bond with the Hyderabadi culture and traditions, the period of which extends over a period of more than one hundred years.

I do not know at what auspicious moment my foundation was laid or what prayers were chanted at that time, that I am not only housing seven generations of the same family for the last one hundred and more years, but I have also acquired such a character that an entire epoch is identified by my name.

My construction was completed in the year 1899. The date-reckoning couplet composed was:

'Khana bagh Aziz Jung hai khoob
Hai makeen Saheb-e-viqar wo tameez
Arz kar aye Mu'een saal bina
Hai makaane Aziz bagh aziz"

The last line reckons the date 1317 H. corresponding to 1899 A.D., according to the Abjad account of Arabic alphabets.

My foundation was laid by Shamsul Ulema Nawab Aziz Jung Villa. Aziz Jung, by the way, did not belong to the aristocracy of Hyderabad. He was a self-made, hardworking, learned man and a research scholar of high standard. The nineteenth century aristocracy of Hyderabad formed an easy-going, care-free culture. The Nawabs (nobles) led a pompous and luxurious life. Their life style was more inclined to vanity and outward show. Utility was given secondary importance in their life.

Hazrath Villa, my Founder, was no doubt influenced to a great extent by the prevailing standard of life in Hyderabad. Yet, he had in his view the negative aspects of this life style too. From the beginning he had the sense of making motley of both aesthetic and functional aspects of a building. He attached basic importance to conduct and character. He kept in his view the realities and inspirations in my shaping. When character and concepts are clubbed with bricks and mortar of a building, the real personality of the building comes out clearly.

As a matter of fact the buildings under my name are neither spacious, nor very attractive from the point of view of architecture (The reputed Architect, Janab Anwar Aziz, a Member of the INTACH Award Committee may not agree with me in this respect). What is unique is my special character.

When the house was founded, a mosque was also built adjacent to it.

Within my premises was written a book, 'kaasht-e-angoor' (Book on cultivation of grapes), almost 100 years back. Within my premises experiments were conducted on cultivation of grapes, which formed the basis for introduction of grape cultivation on large scale after the formation of the State of Andhra Pradesh.

Within my premises was written a book, 'Hayatul Hamam', a book on pigeons' lives, their species, diseases and cure. It is the only book of its kind in Urdu language. Special 'pigeons houses' were built for the pigeons which not only added to my beauty, but also assigned to me individuality.

Within my premises was written the great voluminous dictionary in the Persian language which runs into 17 volumes and 10,000 pages. Yet, it was compiled up to the alphabet '*Jeem*' only and was never completed even by any Institution.

Within my premises were compiled collections of Revenue Codes, of which a number of editions were later published and which form an integral part of Reference Collections in Revenue offices and the courts of law, even today. Recently, Mr. Pratap Reddy, a senior advocate argued in the A.P. High Court on the basis of these Codes.

From my premises were sent Persian and Urdu manuscripts and books to the Royal Asiatic Society, Calcutta, Board of Examiners, Calcutta, Mohammedan College, Aligarh, Madrasa Aliya, Calcutta, Islamic Library, Madras during the period 1907 to 1911. 'Pustak Dan', donation of books is continued until now. Urdu libraries were established after 1954 in four foreign countries; Japan, Israel, Russia and Czechoslovakia.

From my premises were conducted relief works for the victims of the Musi Floods of 1908. Free medicines were supplied from my premises during the spread of the worldwide flu pandemic. Free distribution of medicines still continues in some form or other. 'Health for All' provides medical aid to poor and needy patients.

Within my premises you find the rain-gauge functioning for the last 90 years, which is a unique feature in a house hold environment. Within my premises were started movements of social reforms and abolition of un-Islamic orthodox, customs and rituals.

Within my premises was conducted a famous and momentous research work, 'Tareekhun Nawayat' (History of Nawayat) about which Moulana Shibli said, "The kind of information Nawab sahib has provided in this book on the events and happenings, is the first of its own kind in this respect. We commend the research done by Nawab sahib and hope all countries in the world will recognize the value of this rare kind of work".

Within my premises the laborious work of the first Urdu word counting was done which was released by the then Prime Minister Indira Gandhi at her residence. Sixty-two books were published by Villa Academy to date.

It is true that a country acquires good name on account of the noble character of its citizens. Likewise, a building is also known by the characters and conduct of its members. Read! What does Khaja Altaf Hussain Hali says about Hazrath Villa:

"Courage, hardworking, punctuality, management skill, avoiding trivialities, adopting good manners, cleanliness and such other qualities as are found in him, are rarely found in others."

When Khwaja Hasan Nizami visited me in June, 1929, he wrote in his diary, "It is amazing all the four brothers live in a single house with mutual love and unity. I have seen such unanimity very rarely. This is a model house in which cleanliness of high standard is found. If someone has a sensitive heart, as soon as he enters, he is bound to have the feeling he entered a house of five hundred years back, a house of a true and devoted Muslim. In short this house is example for those who want to progress in modern life maintaining at the same time the glory of Islam".

On May 2, 1942, His Majesty, the King of Hyderabad, Nizam the VII gave me the honor of paying a visit. He expressed his views about me and my residents in Persian in a local daily. He said thus, "On such noble traits of characters and conduct only (as are found in the residents of Aziz Bagh), the Civilization of the East can be proud of".

On December 4, 1961, His Excellency, the Governor of A.P., Mr. Bhimsen Sachar, in his presidential speech at a function of 'Villa Day' held at Urdu Hall, pointing towards the family members residing within my premises said, "How lucky are these people who are sitting in front of me. They belong to a family and live in a house, which is an example to every Indian, or I think, for every human being". (Subras, Urdu journal, Villa number, 1962).

Mr. Shankar Dayal Sharma, then Governor of A.P., in his presidential speech at a function of Villa Academy, lauded my character and literary services.

The reason why I had such a glorious past is because I always represented the bright aspects of Hyderabad and guided towards higher values of life, displaying at the same time exemplary character of my own. I opted for a moderate way of life. If the same fundamental characters continue, who is there who will not believe in my bright future?

Introduction

The city of Hyderabad has a rich History of 400 glorious years. The city is multi-ethnic, and is richly gifted with a variety of cultures. The city presents an attractive combination of old world charm along with potential growth opportunity.

The history of Hyderabad begins with the establishment of the Qutub Shahi dynasty since 1512 that is well-known as a fortress city of Golconda. Inadequacy of water and frequent epidemics of plague and cholera persuaded Mohammed, the fifth Quli Qutub Shahi ruler to venture outward to establish the new city with the Charminar at its center and with four great roads fanning out in the four important directions.

Hyderabad's fame, strategic location and Golconda's legendary wealth attracted the Mughals who captured Golconda after a long blockade in 1687. After this defeat the importance of Hyderabad declined to some extent and the city fell into partial ruin.

Mir Qamaruddin, the son of an able officer of Aurangzeb was a favorite of the emperor. He served as a minister under the Mughal emperor Muhammad Shah and was conferred with the title of Asif Jah. Consequently he rose to the post of the Viceroy of Deccan while still very young. After Mohammed Shah's death, Mir Qamaruddin assumed the title of Nizam-ul-Mulk and declared himself as a sovereign prince. This led to the establishment of the Asif Jahi dynasty, named after the title of its founder, 'Asif Jah'.

The Asif Jahi dynasty spanned 224 years, seven generations from A.D. 1724 to 1948, a period much longer than the Qutub Shahi Dynasty which lasted 171 years. The state covered an extensive 95,337 sq. miles, an area larger than Mysore or Gwalior and the size of Nepal and Kashmir put together. With the diversity of languages, total size and various cultures, Hyderabad gained a nationwide importance under the Asif Jahi dynasty of the Nizams.

The content of this book spans 110 years of 'Aziz Bagh' history located within the old City of Hyderabad.

When my wife Razia went to the Naperville Public Library in search of a book on Indian culture, she accidentally stumbled upon a book called, 'Indian Style' by Suzanne Slasin and Stafford Cliff. When she further explored the book, she saw a picture of 'Aziz Bagh'. She brought this book home to show me. That is when it occurred to me that it took a foreigner of European descent to discover my ancestral home called, Aziz Bagh, while I have sat around doing nothing. It spontaneously occurred to me that I must do something and take it upon myself to do full justice to this rich cultural and historical heritage home. Seven generations have lived in this house since it was built 110 years ago.

The outcome of this book is my genuine effort to represent the Aziz Bagh culture with accuracy and sincerity. I have learned a lot about this place while growing up, listening to my elders talk about it and from various publications about this house.

Since its construction in 1899, Aziz Bagh has propelled into Cultural Heritage status. Aziz Bagh was presented with the most prestigious 'INTACH' (Indian National Trust for Art and Cultural Heritage) on July 27, 1997. This award is presented to well-maintained structures.

It is hoped that this book will offer a great deal to many people including readers, readers abroad, old and young alike. It offers a chance to recollect, pass on a heritage, and explore a rich legacy. To the researcher it is a source book. To the visitor it is a guide-book, and to most people it is culture and history. To the historian it offers a diverse, but logical look at the past. In summary it is a treasure.

On behalf of myself and all the members of the Aziz Jung family, I would like to thank the readers and hope that this book will be both informative and a great source of reference.

This book is intended to introduce everyone to the distinguished culture, academic achievements, historical events, and traditions of the Aziz Jung kinfolk. It is intended to inspire pride among all members of the Aziz Jung family and my distinguished readers. The information presented here is as accurate as the sources available to the Author. To further clarify, the source is none other than the individuals who grew up in the Aziz Bagh environment. This book is not about comparison of personalities. Read it with an open mind and enjoy.

Finally, it would have been impossible to work from the other end of the globe in the United States without the teamwork of my very knowledgeable family members. Any errors and omissions are unintentional and they will be rectified upon request in the next edition. Errors and omissions if any are neither intentional nor personal but probably due to lack of proper resources. It was impossible for the author to include each and every ones' biographies because it was not the intention of this book or its scope.

Chapter 1

All About Aziz Bagh

Before and during the Aziz Bagh construction, the house opposite Aziz Bagh was the temporary residence of Nawab Aziz Jung. This temporary house was later bought by Ahmed Jalili and became known as 'Jalil Manzil'.

Aziz Bagh was built in 1899 with the sale proceeds of books authored by Ahmed Abdul Aziz, Khan Bahadur Shams-ul-Ulaima Nawab Aziz Jung Villa. Aziz Jung's books were very well written they were always in demand.

Asif-ul-Lughat, the Farsi (Persian)-Urdu dictionary in 17 Volumes, although incomplete due to Aziz Jung's ill-health was one of the best sellers both in Hyderabad and in Iran. Unfortunately Aziz Jung passed away in 1924 before completing the volume. The last published volume was in 1922. In the early '60 some Irani scholars came to Hyderabad and displayed interest in the Asif-ul Lughat Volumes.

Out of the total twenty-nine books that Aziz Jung authored, twenty-seven were published during his lifetime. All books were very popular.

Aziz Bagh, surrounded by beautiful landscape.

Aziz Bagh is one of the two houses given representation in the prestigious illustrated book 'Indian Style' by Suzanne Slasin and Stafford Cliff. The caption for the picture reads, "Artistic Center," and Aziz Bagh is introduced as follows: Built in 1899 in the suburbs of Hyderabad, the house has always been a center for writers and artists. Dr. Hasanuddin Ahmed, an administrator and scholar, whose grandfather built the house, is a member of the Nawayat family, a clan of Arab origin who came to India more than 700 years ago and settled on the western coast.

Cultural heritage is the legacy of physical and intangible attributes of a group or society that are inherited from past generations, maintained in the present, and bestowed for the benefit of future generations.

Seven generations lived on the estate, which includes outbuildings and the once housed printing presses. The main residence is a curious vernacular mixture of Neoclassical and Gothic Revival styles.

On the exterior, pointed-arched openings flank an impressive Ionic-columned portico. In the interior, fretted windows, some with stained glass and polished marble floors form a backdrop for a collection of Anglo-Indian Victorian heirlooms.

As a famous writer describes, "The house of Aziz Jung has many titles to fame: famous for its modality, famous for its learning, famous for its elegant taste, special culture, and administrative achievements. In short from points of principles and rules of live the house is an institution unto itself.

A remarkable feature of this house is that the off-shoots of the family tree are all men and women of integrity endowed with organizing ability, all well placed on the rung of life. The Aziz Bagh named after Aziz Jung is a miniature colony, fringed on all sides by a tribe of near kith and kin."

The neighborhood Noorkhan Bazaar Sultanpura was developed by Nawab Aziz Jung. The adjoining locality is called Bazaar Nurul Umra or Noorkhan Bazaar. The Road in front of Aziz Bagh is named as Aziz Jung Road, recorded in the Municipal Corporation of Hyderabad Deccan.

The worst flood of Hyderabad Deccan in the year 1908 was no match for the elevated, strong and sturdy construction of Aziz Bagh which was only nine years old at the time. Now 110 years later it is still strong and in the same original condition.

The Aziz Bagh family in United States - 1

Chicago, IL, 5th August, 2005.

The Aziz Bagh family in United States - 2

Chicago, IL, 19th May 2006.

Aziz-ul-Akhbaar Published from Aziz Bagh:
The journal Aziz-ul-Akhbaar was published by Nawab Aziz Jung from Aziz Bagh around 1902.

Community Health:
When the influenza broke out in the early 1940's in an epidemic form, Deen Yar Jung set up a Health Camp. He immediately made arrangements to isolate the healthy population and situated them in a separate camp. This camp supplied medication and food for the sick. Numerous sick individuals were treated who would otherwise have died due to the severe spread of the infectious disease.

Red-light District Elimination Project:
A *red-light district* is a neighborhood or a part of a neighborhood where illegal businesses connected to the adult population take place with women being the innocent victims. When Deen Yar Jung was the City Commissioner of Police of Hyderabad during 1944, he enforced strict orders to suppress the brothels. With the help of raids this social evil was eliminated to a great extent.

He started a program to relocate unfortunate victims of the 'Red-Light District'. First he banned the 'Red-Light District', and then provided the innocent victimized women with alternative jobs that satisfied their financial needs in a respectful manner. 'Women Welfare' was established to assist the victims of the brothel.

UNICEF (United Nations International Children's Emergency Fund):
In collaboration with the UNICEF, a branch of UNO in India, and with the cooperation of the ICSW (Indian Council of Social Work) milk supplies were distributed to hundreds of children daily from Aziz Bagh in the late '50s.

Anees H. Ahmed was the General Secretary of the ICSW and with her dedication and perseverance, this effort was made possible. For many years young children formed a line every morning to get their share of a cup of milk.

Red Cross: The Indian Red Cross's programs are grouped into four main core areas: Promoting humanitarian principles and values; Disaster response; Disaster preparedness; and Health and Care in the Community. Anees H. Ahmed volunteered tirelessly assisting the war victims providing them with food, clothing and medications.

Villa Academy:
Villa Academy has published numerous books since it was established in 1962 by Dr. Hasanuddin Ahmed. Education is a priority for all the members of the Aziz Jung family.

Many books have been published and formally released on a regular basis by learned and high ranking officials. Through education an interaction is developed, and the brain is trained to reason and develop in a constructive manner. In its technical sense education is the process by which society deliberately transmits its acquired knowledge, values, and skills from one generation to another.

Food for All Program:
Every year food supplies are distributed to the needy families. This is made possible by concerned Aziz Bagh family members. Since this program's inception in 1992, the number of contributors has increased each year. Last year 16 years later 125 portions were distributed.

Grocery supplies are stored in Aziz Bagh for humanitarian distribution. 2009

Grocery supplies are stored in Aziz Bagh for humanitarian distribution. 2008

Everyone participate in their annual social and moral obligations by giving our share of charity, whether it is for educational assistance, helping a deserving person get married, or even helping someone with basic necessities such as food.

If someone wants to make a donation, whether small or, they would like to make sure that their donation is well spent, and passed on to the person or family it was intended for. With this concept in mind, the Food for All Program was developed. The items distributed are practical, which ensures that they are consumed by the recipients.

The recipients are chosen in a non-discriminatory manner. Families are chosen that have no working members due to chronic illness, disabilities, etc. Some of them are chronically sick, and cannot work to earn a living. Some families do not ask for charity due to their self-respect and dignity. In such cases contributors step in and go to them instead, with food for at least three months.

Several years later, this program is still ongoing with the help of regular contributions from Aziz Bagh family members.

Education Awareness:
Hidden talent is sought out to be mentored and educated in a systematic manner by Dr. Hasanuddin Ahmed. The concept is that, if one member of a family is educated and gains employment, the entire family has the opportunity to become financially secure. This is an effort to improve the living standard of the community.

Charitable Distributions:
Financial support is regularly provided to the very poor and to unfortunate families where a primary earning member either passed away or is terminally sick. If a head of a family is unable to support the family, Aziz Bagh members are always willing to assist.

Weddings for the Poor and deserving:
Weddings are arranged regularly for many poor and deserving young girls, with the wedding expenses paid by Aziz Bagh family members. This is an ongoing effort to situate young girls where they belong, and to prevent poverty.

Aziz Bagh, a Banquet Hall:
Aziz Bagh, although a family residence, is always there as a 'Banquet Hall', or a' Function Hall, free of charge to poor and needy families if they need a hall for a wedding ceremony. To date, numerous weddings have taken place at Aziz Bagh to accommodate the needs of the deserving.

Artists in the Family:
A professional International Banker, Artist, Calligrapher, Poet, and Scholar, Mr. Aziz Ahmed is a man of many talents. His calligraphy skills are rare and unique, probably one in several thousands. His calligraphy talents are in English as well as in Arabic, Persian, and Urdu.

Erum Ahmed is a Bio-Engineering student at the prestigious Northwestern University in the Chicago area. She is also an artist.

Collector in the Family
Syed Asghar Hussaini has a collection of postage stamps and currency notes. So far he has collected more than a thousand currency notes from 140 countries around the world. His stamp collection includes Indian mint stamps starting from Indian independence in 1947 till date and Great Britain mint stamp from 1968 to the very present. He is also a life member of the Hyderabad philatelic and hobbies society.

Many famous people visited Aziz Bagh

The ruler of Hyderabad Deccan, H.E.H. Nawab Mir Osman Ali Khan the Nizam visited Aziz Bagh twice, once on the occasion of the wedding of Mohammed Hyder and Zehra, (daughter of Nawab Deen Yar Jung), on 1st May 1942, and then upon the death of Mohiuddin Ahmed, 2nd son of Nawab Aziz Jung, in 1944.

H.E.H. the Nizam IV,
Ruler of Hyderabad Deccan.

Sir Mohammed Zafarullah Khan

Governor Mir Akber Ali Khan

Governor Ali Yaver Jung

Sir Arthur Lothian British Resident and Nawab of Chittari, visited Aziz Bagh on the occasion of the wedding of Ahmeduddin Siddiqui, son in law of Nawab Deen Yar Jung, on 23rd November 1945.

Sir Mirza Ismail and Sir Mohammed Zafarullah Khan, along with high ranking Police Officials visited Aziz Bagh on 22nd January 1947.

Sir Nizamath Jung visited to grace the wedding reception of Dr. Hasanuddin Ahmed on 1st May 1947.

Ali Yaver Jung, Governor of Maharashtra, and Barrister Mir Akber Ali Khan, Governor of Uttar Pradesh, were invited by Villa Academy book releases, by various authors including Dr. Hasanuddin Ahmed, in the mid 1960s.

His Excellency K. C. Abraham, Governor of Andhra Pradesh visited on the occasion of the author's wedding reception on 2nd January 1979.

Governor K.C. Abraham

Governor Krishna Kant

Nawab of Chittari

Chief Justice of Andhra Pradesh High Court and His Excellency, Krishna Kant, former Governor of Andhra Pradesh and former Vice President of India, visited Aziz Bagh on the occasion of Samiha's wedding in December 1996.

His Excellency Shankar Dayal Sharma was invited to one of Dr. Hasanuddin Ahmed's book release.

Chapter 2

Did You Know?

Aziz Bagh was honored with the most prestigious award 'INTACH', Indian National Trust for Art and Cultural Heritage on July 27, 1997. This award is presented to well-maintained structures. Credit goes to Anees H. Ahmed and Shamsuddin Ahmed for the maintenance of Aziz Bagh on a regular basis.

The first member of our family to have travelled the world was Mohiuddin Ahmed, Nawab Aziz Jung's 2nd son in 1935.

Aziz Bagh was built in 1899 and is still standing in the same condition for the past 110 years later.

Dr. and Mrs. Hasanuddin Ahmed celebrated their 50th Wedding Anniversary on 1st May 1997 at Aziz Bagh and they were married on 1st May 1947 at Aziz Bagh.

Dr. and Mrs. Hasanuddin Ahmed in 1972.

After Police Action the first Prime Minister of India, Jawaharlal Nehru, requested Deen Yar Jung to accept a senior assignment, but he declined the offer on the grounds that he served one master and was loyal to the Nizam and hence could not serve the Indian Government with the same enthusiasm.

Dr. Hamid Hussain, son of Yousuf Hussain and grandson of Aziz Jung, was honored with O.B.E (Order of British Empire), the most prestigious British award.

Dr. Hasanuddin Ahmed and Dr. Hamid Hussain, OBE,
with the Mayor of Rotherham, UK, 2006.

Among Aziz Jung's twelve children his second son Mohiuddin Ahmed was the first child to pass away in 1944 and his fourth daughter Aijazunissa Begum who survived all other siblings until she passed away in 2004.

Date of Death
12th August 1944

Date of Death
19h December 2004

Aziz Jung's first grandchild is Shehzadi Begum born to his first daughter Azizunnisa in 1905.

Aziz Jungs's last grandchild Syed Asghar Hussaini born to fourth daughter Aijazunnisa Begum in 1953.

The Aziz Bagh, 'Summer Retreat'.

Aziz Bagh is the home to seven generations starting with Mohammed Nizamuddin Ahmed, Aziz Jung's father, since it was built in 1899. Mohammed Nizamuddin lived in Aziz Bagh only one year until he died in 1900. Aziz Jung was very attached to his father and always took care of him as a first born child.

Chapter 3

Tareeq-un-Nawayat
(Family Profile Section)

GENEALOGY

Ahmed Abdul Aziz, Khan Bahadur Shams-Ul-Ulaima Nawab Aziz Jung Villa's genealogical line connects him with Hazrat Abdullah Bin Jaffar-e-Tayyar, and Hazrat Zainab, the daughter of Ali bin Abu Talib.

He traces the genealogy of his family, in his book 'Kulyat-e-Nizam' in the 'Hayat-ul-Aziz' chapter as follows:

According to Aziz Jung's research, the family of Nawayat originally hails from Medina. They migrated to Baghdad. Later they migrated from Baghdad to Basra in 752 H. (1351 CE) and then to various ports on the Western coast of South India in 770 H (1368 CE) and later.

Sayyidana Jaffar-e-Tayyar
Abdullah-ul-Akbar-ul-Jawwad
Ali Al-Zainabi
Mohammed-ul-Idrees
Ibrahim-ul-Arabi
Jaffar-us-Syed
Mohammed-ul-Alam
Dawood
Abdullah
Ahmed
Ibrahim
Abu Rijal Hafiz Ahmed Durwish
Hafiz Mohammed Abdul Qadir
Mohammed Abdullah Mohammed Idrees, died - 1199 H (1784 CE)

Mohammed Abdullah, Commander, Ongole Fort
Mohammed Hussain
Mohammed Nizamuddin Judge, City Civil Court, Hyderabad Deccan. *(Mohammed Nizamuddin had three sons, Ahmed Abdul Aziz, Mohammed Ahmedullah, and Ahmed Abdul Wadud.)*
Ahmed Abdul Aziz, (Aziz Jung Bahadur) He was a poet, author of several books, administrator (Revenue Officer) and social activist.

Aziz Jung's Descendents Genealogy will be continued in the next publication:

'Aziz Jung Heritage Genealogy Tree'

More than 550 descendents are identified.

The Aziz Bagh 'Summer Retreat', close up.

Chapter 4

Glimpses of the Aziz Jung Clan

Moulvi Mohammed Nizamuddin, died 1900,
Justice, City Civil Court: Father of Nawab Aziz Jung.

Moulvi Mohammed Nizamuddin was born at Nellore. He was grandson of Mohammed Abdullah, Commander of the Ongole Fort. He was a very learned individual and was a Judge High Court at Nellore. Later he reluctantly accepted the post of the District Superintendent of Police, Nellore. Since he was not interested in pursuing a career with the Police department, he resigned soon afterwards and joined the Madrasa-e-Azam as Professor at Madras. He was more inclined towards an Academic career. A Madrasa (قسردم) in Arabic is any educational institution. He was also a well known Qur'an scholar.

The Qutub Shahi Dynasty ruled Hyderabad Deccan for 171 years. As the Mughal Empire was declining and began to split up, and at the same time the

Qutub Shahi Dynasty was at its turbulent stage, the Mughal Viceroy Asif Jah-I proclaimed himself the Nizam and established independent rule of the Hyderabad Deccan. Hyderabad once again became a major capital city, ruled by successive Nizams of the Asaf Jah dynasty.

Mir Qamaruddin assumed the title of Nizam-ul-Mulk and conducted himself as an independent prince. This led to the establishment of the Asif Jahi dynasty. The Asif Jahi dynasty spanned seven generations from A.D. 1724 to 1948, a period much longer than the preceding Qutub Shahis. The state covered an extensive 95,337 sq. miles, an area larger than Mysore or Gwalior and the size of Nepal and Kashmir put together.

Basheer Bagh Palace was just built by Sir Asman Jah. First adhesive stamps were just issued. The Nizam's State Railway had just then established and opened to public. The Municipal Corporation of Hyderabad had organized cannon fire at 4:30 AM, 12:00 Noon and 8:00 PM. to inform the public about time.

Around the year 1870 Hyderabad was in a process of modernizing and Mir Mahboob Ali Khan, the Nizam VI was in dire need of dedicated, learned and effective administrators. Sir Salar Jung was the Prime Minister of Hyderabad during the period of Mir Mahboob Ali Khan, Nizam VI. Sir Salar Jung was the father of Salar Jung III, the famous Salar Jung Museum founder. He took upon himself to find talented administrators for Hyderabad. Sir Salar Jung died in 1883 at an early age of 54.

During this significant time, in 1870 Mohammed Nizamuddin migrated to Hyderabad along with his three sons Ahmed Abdul Aziz, Mohammed Ahmedullah and Ahmed Abdul Wadud.

At first he accepted a position with the revenue Department, but he was quickly recognized by Sir Salar Jung and with his proven capabilities, he was offered a position as Justice City Civil Court Hyderabad.

Mohammed Nizamuddin lived with his three sons Ahmed Abdul Aziz (Aziz Jung), Mohammed Ahmedullah and Ahmed Abdul Wadud at the house opposite the present house Aziz Bagh before it was built, until 1899. Ahmed Abdul Wadud was Autistic and was misunderstood as mentally disturbed. In those days Autism was not properly researched.

Mohammed Nizamuddin died in 1900 at the newly built Aziz Bagh. Same year his grandson Ruknuddin Ahmed was born.

Ahmed Abdul Aziz Khan Bahadur Shams-ul-Ulema
Nawab Aziz Jung Villa, born 1860 - died 1924.

Left: Aliuddin Ahmed, (Nawab Deen Yar Jung Bahadur),
born 1893 - died 1964. Right: Dr. Hasanuddin Ahmed,
Indian Administrative Service and Chairman Minorities Commission.

The Sustainer of Aziz Bagh, Shamsuddin Ahmed

Shamsuddin Ahmed and his wife Farzana.

Left to Right; Ruknuddin Ahmed, Dr. Hasanuddin Ahmed and Shamsuddin Ahmed.

Chapter 5

Aziz Jung Family Tree

Ahmed Abdul Aziz, Nawab Aziz Jung

Aziz Jung was born on 28th September 1860 in Nellore, a District of Madras State, India, where his father Nizamuddin Ahmed was the District Judge. Nellore district was in the southern part of Madras State situated on the northern bank of Pennar River. This district became part of the state of Andhra Pradesh in 1956 when the states were reorganized on a linguistic basis. Until 1953, it was a part of the composite Madras State.

A portion of the family cemetery is also in the Nellore District. During the early 1960s Aziz Jung's grandsons, Dr. Hasanuddin Ahmed and Ahmed Abdul Aziz (Asif) visited the ancestral cemetery at Nellore and identified most of the family graves. This is an example of the enthusiasm and concern of the Aziz Jung's descendants with regard to his family, both living and dead. Aziz Jung came to Hyderabad in 1870 from Nellore with his father and two younger brothers Mohammed Ahmedullah and Ahmed Abdul Wadud when he was ten years old.

Mohammed Ahmedullah:

Mohammed Ahmedullah was Aziz Jung's younger brother who passed away at a young age and left behind three sons, Mohammed Habibullah, Mohammed Asadullah, and Mohammed Valiullah. Aziz Jung brought up his three nephews as his own children, and they were later married to three of Aziz Jung's daughters. Since Mohammed Ahmedullah passed away at a young age, not much is known about his life in detail. His three sons being all educated sufficiently, indicates that Mohammed Ahmedullah did provide the basic foundation to his three sons.

Ahmed Abdul Wadud:

Ahmed Abdul Wadud was the youngest brother of Aziz Jung. He was Autistic. Autism was not researched in those days and as a result Ahmed Abdul Wadud was misunderstood as being mentally ill. On the contrary he was a genius whose advice was constantly sought by many believers. Aziz Jung recognized his condition and closely supervised and monitored him with special care. Some family members thought that he had a mental condition. Ahmed Abdul Wadud was very quiet and always minded his own business.

Although Aziz Jung started his career in Hyderabad as Revenue Officer, he resigned from this position to pursue a career in poetry and literature. During his life time he authored more books than most people read in their lifetime.

Aziz Jung wrote 29 books on a variety of subjects, including agriculture, chronography, eulogy, finance, history, law, lexicon, literature, martyrdom, religion, rhetorics, and numerous poems in Farsi (Persian) and Urdu.

Aziz Jung had many great qualities. Besides being an author, he was a thinker and lover of humanity. He was a reformer and a social worker. He spent a major portion of his life serving the welfare of his fellow man. In recognition of his services he was granted a permanent Free Railway Pass (Silver Pass) for first class travel. The Governor of Andhra Pradesh, Bhimsen Sachar, rightly remarked that Aziz Jung can be reckoned among the great men of India. He was one of the persons who made Hyderabad, "The Hyderabad".

Books Authored by Aziz Jung:

S. No:	Name of the book:	Topic:	Language:	Year Published:
1	Unmadat ul Qawanin	Selected Laws	Urdu	1889
2	Azamul Atiyat	Inam Code	Urdu	1889
3	Tarkari Ki Kasht	Agriculture	Urdu	1901
4	Atiyat-e-Asafi	Inam Code	Urdu	1902
5	Tareeq-un-Nawayat *	History of the Nawayats	Urdu	1904
6	Falhatul Nakhl	Agriculture	Urdu	1904
7	Mushtalihat-e-Deccan	Lexicon	Urdu	1904
8	Kasht-e-Angoor	Agriculture	Urdu	1905
9	Asif-ul-Lughat (17 Volumes) **	Lexicon	Persian/Urdu	1905-1922
10	Hayatul Hamam	Ornithology	Urdu	1906
11	Mahboob-ul Seer	History	Persian	1906
12	Shirazae Dafatir	Office Code	Urdu	1907
13	Gharaibul Jumal	Chronography	Urdu	1908
14	Atiyat-e-Sultani	Inam Code	Urdu	1908
15	Kulyat-e-Nizam-e-Villa	Poems	Persian	1910
16	Kulyat-e-Nizam-e-Villa	Poems	Urdu	1910
17	Majmoo-e-Qawanin-e-Malguzari (5 Volumes)	Revenue Code	Urdu	1911
18	Sadar Mjomo-e-Qawanin-Malwo Hisab	Financial Code	Urdu	1913
19	Khazina-e-Finance Wo Hisab	Financial Code	Urdu	1913
20	Al Tanis-wal-Tazkir	Rhetoric	Urdu	1919
21	Meary-e-Fasahat	Rhetoric	Urdu	1919
22	Tasveer-e-Noor	Eulogy of Prophet	Urdu	1920
23	Tasveer-e-Balaghat	Eulogy of Prophet	Persian	1922
24	Dastan-e-Gham of Husain	Martyrdom	Persian	1923
25	Siyaq-e-Deccan	Accounting	Urdu	Not Known
26	Villa-e-Hafiz in the style of Hafiz	Collection of Poems	Persian	1974***
27	Villa-e-Pakan	Eulogy of Prophet	Persian	Unpublished
28	Natya Kalam-e-Villa	Eulogy of Prophet	Persian	Unpublished
29	Nazar-e-Sultan	****	Urdu	Unpublished
I	Lisan-ul Hind-Wal Ajam+	Rhetorics	Urdu	Monthly
II	Azizul Akhbaar +	Improved Agriculture	Urdu	Monthly

*Tareeq-un-Nawayat is translated with modifications by G. M. Mahajir in, N.Y., USA in 2009.
**17 Volumes of Asif-ul-Lughat were done, but the dictionary is still incomplete due to his ill-health. This dictionary although incomplete, it was one if his most popular and best seller in Hyderabad and in Iran.
*** Poetry, published in 1974 by Dr. Hasanuddin Ahmed.
****Gifts (Nazar) were presented to the kings on special occasion; Aziz Jung wrote a book on this *subject.*
+Aziz Jung also edited two monthly journals.

Aziz Bagh, the Heritage of Culture.

Aziz Jung was a man of principles and he made sure that his children followed in his footsteps.

Aziz Jung's younger brother Mohammed Ahmedullah passed away at a young age. He was survived by three young sons, Mohammed Habibullah, Mohammed Asadullah and Mohammed Valiullah. Aziz Jung took the responsibility to raise his young nephews along with his own children. Later on these young men were married to three of Aziz Jung's own daughters.

Aziz Jung's personal living area within Aziz Bagh was on the 1st floor area on the East side of the building, presently occupied by his great grandson Shamsuddin Ahmed.

Ghazi Yar Jung lived in the portion next to the tennis court. This building was detached from the main Aziz Bagh portion but within the compound.

Mohiuddin Ahmed lived in another building within the compound, where Ruknuddin Ahmed moved after the death of his brother Mohiuddin Ahmed.

Both Deen Yar Jung and Ruknuddin Ahmed lived in the West wing of Aziz Bagh main building.

Aziz Jung passed away on 17th October 1924. He was survived by four sons and eight daughters. All four of his sons held positions of distinction in which they established themselves credibly and earned great popularity by virtue of excellent character, humanism and philanthropic activities. Three of his grand children were born during his life, Zehra Hyder, Hasanuddin Ahmed, and Razia Siddiqui.

Aziz Jung and his sons:

From L to R: Aliuddin Ahmed (Deen Yar Jung), Ghaziuddin Ahmed (Ghazi Yar Jung), Aziz Jung, Mohiuddin Ahmed, and Ruknuddin Ahmed, 1917.

Aziz Bagh, the Heritage of Culture.

Ghaziuddin Ahmed, Ghazi Yar Jung

b 1879 - d 1960

Ghaziuddin Ahmed, Ghazi Yar Jung

Ghazi Yar Jung was the first son of Aziz Jung Bahadur. He was married to Anwari Begum, they had no children..

He was Judge of the Hyderabad High Court. After his retirement, Ghazi Yar Jung held the office of a Minister in the 'Paigah' of Sir Vicar for several years.

Though he was born with a silver spoon, Ghazi Yar Jung led a very ascetic life. He was a simple, devout God fearing and pious man.
He created a trust, called Wakf Baitul Madina, in the year 1942. Deen Yar Jung succeeded him as the Mutawalli (managing trustee). He was succeeded by Dr. Hasanuddin Ahmed in 1964. Dr. Hasanuddin Ahmed developed the property under Government of India Scheme for development of Urban Wakf properties. Scholarships are given to merited students in addition to monthly aid to widows, medical and marriage aid.

Dr. Hasanuddin Ahmed has resigned his position as managing trustee due to his busy academic and social activities, and has been succeeded by his son Shamsuddin Ahmed.

Ghaziuddin Ahmed, Ghazi Yar Jung was known to be very strict and a disciplinarian. He never compromised when discipline was concerned. Being a Judge by profession, he expected equality justice for all. As the eldest brother of four brothers, and eight sisters, he was always respected and taken seriously. Likewise, being the eldest brother, he maintained a certain level of dignity and made it clear that he was in charge. Although very firm, he was a kind man beneath.

His favorite fruit was mango. In the mango season, one would never find him without a mango. Among great qualities of all Aziz Jung children, they all had their own personalities. Some appeared very mild and some very serious, but they were all educated, brilliant, highly qualified and very gentle individuals. They were all well placed professionally.

He passed away on 18th December 1960. Ghazi Yar Jung is remembered as a mentor to his younger siblings. He was respected by all and had high expectations for his juniors. He was married, but had no children.

Mohiuddin Ahmed

b 1880 – d 1944

Mohiuddin Ahmed

Mohiuddin Ahmed was the second son of Aziz Jung Bahadur. He was the Commissioner of Customs. He was well known for his administrative talents, legal knowledge and integrity. He was married to Tayaba Begum and they had no children.

He visited Chicago in 1935, likely making him one of the few Hyderabadis to have visited Chicago in the 1930s. He is remembered by his family as a very funny and loving person. He had a remarkable sense of humor and always tried to make people happy. His cheerful personality was his identity.

Mohiuddin Ahmed had a mild temperament. He seldom got upset, and if he did get upset for some reason, he would quickly remedy the situation with his well mannered, spontaneous loving and humorous approach.

He was a favorite of his nieces and nephews. Having no children of his own, he adopted his most favorite niece Ruqhia, daughter of his younger brother Aliuddin Ahmed, Deen Yar Jung. Upon his return from Chicago, he brought back a 'Gramophone Record', recorded in his own voice, for his favorite niece Ruqhia.

He had a great individual taste for quality. He always procured the best, and never compromised quality for price. He loved to travel, and as such travelled the world in the early '1930s.

Mohiuddin Ahmed continued the tradition of reading the 'Sarapa' written by his father Aziz Jung. This tradition was continued by his younger brother Ruknuddin Ahmed, and it is still continued by Ahmed Abdul Aziz every year.

The children of Aziz Jung had individual qualities of their own. Mohiuddin Ahmed, in spite of occupying a very high position as Commissioner of Customs, never displayed any arrogance. He was kind and very considerate to the less fortunate. He preferred to give than to take away.

To summarize, Mohiuddin Ahmed was an angel with a very humble personality. Although he was high up with a very successful career, he was still 'down to earth'.

He died on 12th August 1944. He was 64 years old and left a very loving memory. He was a man with dignity, self respect and caring character. Such people only come to this world occasionally.

Aliuddin Ahmed, Deen Yar Jung

b 1893 – d 1964

Nawab Deen Yar Jung was the third son of Nawab Aziz Jung Bahadur.

Nawab Deen Yar Jung was born on 26 September, 1893 in Hyderabad at the house across from Aziz Bagh where his father Aziz Jung used to live before the Aziz Bagh was built. He was married on April 11, 1919 to Fatima Begum, daughter of Dr. Fakhiuddin Hussain, a Civil Surgeon of Khurshid Jahi Paigah. Fatima Begum had a twin sister, and one younger brother.

He worked at various districts of the Nizam's Dominion in the Judicial and Revenue Departments and as a District Collector. He also served as the Director of Ecclesiastical Department for a number of years.

On 6 June, 1944 Nawab Deen Yar Jung took over as Commissioner of Police. He was the Director General of City Police during a critical period of Hyderabad's history before and after Police Action in 1948. For his valuable services to the State he was awarded the title of Deen Yar Jung, and received the Asafia Gold Medal on 11th May, 1948.

Deen Yar Jung

Fatima Begum

Deen Yar Jung had a large circle of associates from diverse social, political and religious affiliations.

Deen Yar Jung's Mother:
Deen Yar Jung's mother Amtulla Begum was the youngest daughter of Mohammed Abdul Khudus Chida, an employee of the Revenue Department of Hyderabad. Amtulla Begum had two older siblings, a brother Abdul Aziz Chida and a sister Ismatunissa Begum. She also belonged to the same family tree as Deen Yar Jung's father Aziz Jung. Aziz Jung was married to Amtulla Begum in the year 1889, when he was the Assistant Secretary of the Revenue Department. She died on 25th April 1933.

Individual Character: Deen Yar Jung was a typical representative of an outstanding personality one may be proud of. He represented the Eastern traditions with dignity. He was sophisticated in behavior and was an exceptionally well-mannered individual. He was courteous to everyone. In spite of his extremely busy schedule, he found the time to pay attention to any one that approached him irrespective of their social or economic status, particularly if they were in need of help. He was a man of ethics. The exigencies of administration sometimes made him assume a firm external appearance, but in reality he was very soft, kind hearted and considerate, even to the point of occasionally being exploited by unscrupulous persons.

Deen Yar Jung with Nawab of Chittari among others.

He had opponents as all serious administrators have, but it is a fact that even the worst of his enemies had no grievance against him for having been harmed in any way, but for not having been benefitted adequately or to his own satisfaction. He commanded respect from all around him and inspired confidence among his subordinates. He was a great disciplinarian himself, and expected discipline by his personal example and behavior rather than by mere precepts. He was punctual, worked long hours and was systematic in his habits.

In all his dealings, Deen Yar Jung commanded respect and admiration, and inspired confidence. He was known for his taste in good clothes. He was one of the best dressed men in town.

Deen Yar Jung held an important assignment during critical period in the History of Hyderabad. As mentioned elsewhere in this book, He was the Director General of Police before and immediately after the Police Action. It appeared as though the providence had chosen him to be in charge of the Police Department at the time of this crisis. It goes to his credit that he maintained and strengthened an atmosphere of peace and security for everyone in town. It was due to his administrative ability and statesmanship, and indeed his personal influence that fanaticism from every possible quarter was kept at bay and peace maintained both before and after the duration of the Police Action.

Deen Yar Jung can truly be regarded as a savior of Hyderabad and deserves to be richly honored as such. The main features of his administrative talent lie in his fair-mindedness, quick decision making, sound judgment, robust common sense, power of taking initiative and responsibilities.

Deen Yar Jung as Director General Police.

In summary he was a more distinguished person than the majority of his contemporaries. However, the main characteristic which distinguishes him from the rest is his regard, commitment and faithfulness to his superior, H.E.H., the Nizam.

Group Photo of Deen Yar Jung with His Children, In-Laws, and Grand Children

Standing left to right: Ahmeduddin Siddiqui, Mohammed Hyder, Ruqhia, Aziz Ahmed, Hasanuddin Ahmed, Ahmed Hussain Khan.
Sitting left to right: Razia Siddiqui, Zehra Hyder, Fatima Begum, Aliuddin Ahmed (Deen Yar Jung), Anees H. Ahmed, Soghra Hussain Khan.
Children Standing left to right: Nasreen Ahmed, Masood Hyder, Nisar Hyder, and Miriam Farooq.

Ruqhia Ali's grand Bismillah, 1932.

Deen Yar Jung's two Sons, four Daughters and daughter-in-law:

L to R: Aziz Ahmed, Ruqia M. Ali, Soghra Khan, Mrs. Anees Hasanuddin Ahmed, Razia Siddiqui, Zehra Hyder, and Dr. Hasanuddin Ahmed. 2001.

Deen Yar Jung with his son-in-laws:

L to R: Ahmed Hussain Khan, Mohammed Hyder, Aliuddin Ahmed (Deen Yar Jung), Ahmeduddin Siddiqui and Mahmood Ali.

Sons and Grandsons of Nawab Deen Yar Jung:

Fakhiuddin Ahmed, the first child and son of Deen Yar Jung expired a few hours after birth. He was named after his maternal grandfather. He was buried within the Aziz Bagh compound.

Dr. Hasanuddin Ahmed was a Member of the Indian Administrative Service, Chairman of the Minorities Commission and author of several books. His book Easy Way to the Understanding of the Qur'an was published in United States by Iqra International Educational Publications. All of his books are widely acclaimed worldwide.

Azizuddin Ahmed

Aziz Ahmed, self Portrait.

Aziz U. Ahmed was born on 4th May 1930. He graduated from the Nizam College. He worked briefly with the Eastern Bank Ltd., in Doha Qatar, and later migrated to London, U.K. where he lived until 2007. While in London he worked for Barclays's Bank.

He is a man of many talents. His Calligraphy skills are rare and unique, probably one in several thousands. His Calligraphy talents are both in Latin script as well as in Arabic, Persian, and in Urdu scripts. To be a master in these two entirely different scripts is a work of Art.

Aziz Ahmed 2004.

Dr. Hasanuddin Ahmed, Mohammed Azhar Siddiqui, Aziz Ahmed and Anees Hasanuddin Ahmed, 1973.

Shamsuddin Ahmed

Shamsuddin Ahmed is the great-grandson of Aziz Jung, grandson of Aliuddin Ahmed (Deen Yar Jung) and son of Dr. Hasanuddin Ahmed.

He is a Civil Engineer, a Consultant and Real Estate Property Evaluator.

Shamsuddin Ahmed and Farzana Ahmed.

President of India dines at Dr. Hasanuddin Ahmed's Residence at New Delhi, 1974. Shamsuddin Ahmed is attending to the revered guest.

The daughters of Deen Yar Jung:

Zehra Fatima, the eldest daughter was born on 25th April, 1921. She was educated at the Mahboobia Girls' School, and was married to Mohammed Hyder on 1st May 1942.

Mohammed Hyder was an H.C.S. (Hyderabad Civil Service) officer, District Judge and District Collector. After Indian Independence, he served H.E.H. the Nizam's Trusts Office as Administrator.

They have two sons, Masood Hyder and Nisar Hyder, and one daughter Rizwana Farooq.

Masood Hyder works at the United Nations' World Food Program. He is married to Shahana Hyder. They have three children, Sana, Mohammed, and Nashuan.

Dr. Nisar Hyder has worked as a General Practitioner in Bedford, UK since 1973. He is a partner in a group practice in Bedford. Nisar Hyder is a keen gardener in his spare time. Nisar Hyder is married to Nariman, daughter of Saleema and Ghulam Ahmed, former cricket captain of India, Administrator and Educationist. Nariman has worked as a teacher in Bedford, and is currently an Examiner for Cambridge International Examinations in Islamiyat.

Mariam Hyder-Farooq (born 1977) is married to Nabil Farooq, son of Dr. Faheem and Mariam Farooq. She lives in Boston, U.S.A since her marriage in 2001. She is a graduate from Reading University, U.K and is currently an Assistant Branch Manager at the Milford National Bank and Trust Company.

Faiza Hyder (born 1981) is a graduate from the University of Bedfordshire. She is a teacher by profession. Faiza is a keen and gifted Tennis player and has been captain of her school Tennis team.

Amaan Hyder (born 1982) is a graduate from University College London and gained his M.A from University of East Anglia. He works for Macmillan Publishers in London for their Nature magazine as an Editorial Assistant.

Shaan Hyder (born 1987) is a 4th year Medical student at King's College, London. Shaan is a keen Tennis player and is captain of Tennis team at King's College, London.

Rizwana is married to Saleem Farooq and they have two children, Gehan, and Sabina. Gehan is married to Fernando Demarche, and they have three children, Noe Amar, Ambra Ameena and Ilario Naim.

Razia Fatima, the second daughter was born on 23rd July 1924. She was educated at the Mahboobia Girls' School and was married to Ahmeduddin Siddiqui on 23rd November 1945.

Ahmeduddin Siddiqui was Accountant General for the Government of India, Calcutta. He was son of Nawab Azhar Jung. He passed away in 1961. He is survived by his wife and three children.

They have two daughters Nasreen and Farhana, and one son Mohammed Azhar Siddiqui.

Nasreen is married to Dr. Habib Ahmed and they have two children, Dr. Ali Ahmed and Dr. Yasmin Sitabkhan.

Ali married Dr. Huma. They have four children: Imaan, Zaid, Adil and Yousuf.

Dr. Yasmin married Murtuza Sitabkhan. They have three children: Zain, Adam, and, Riaz.

Farhana is married to Sultan Zia and they have two children, Omar, and Rana. Omar Married Angie, their child: Gabriella Farhana Zia.

Rana married Noman Latif. They have two children: Aydin Zain Latif and Samar Zia Latif

Mohammed Azher Siddiqui married Daisy and they have two children, Raza and Laila.

Soghra Fatima, the third daughter was born on 2nd February 1926. She was educated at the Mahboobia Girls' School, and was married to Ahmed Hussain Khan on 30th November 1945, a week after her sister Razia was married.

Ahmed Hussain Khan, B.Sc, B.E (Manchester University, England) an electrical engineer, was Chief Engineer of the Electricity Board with the Government of Andhra Pradesh.

They have one daughter, Mariam, B.Sc. Substitute Elementary School Teacher, and one son, Abbas Hussain Khan, B.E. self employed.

Mariam is married to Dr. Faheem Farooq, M.B.Ch.B., M.D.. Practicing M.D. in Milford, MA., Instructor in Medicine. They have two children Nabil, M.B.A, works as a Senior V.P. Commercial Lending and Dr. Nihad, Ph.D is Assistant Professor.

Nabil is married to Mariam Hyder-Farooq, B.A. She is Assistant Manager.

Picture taken in 2001 during Nabil's wedding.
L to R Dr. Hasanuddin Ahmed, Nabil Farooq and Aziz Ahmed.

Abbas Hussain Khan is married to Durdana and they have two children Amer and Saba. Saba is married to Ashfaque Ahmed, and they have two children, Rania and Rahil.

Ruqhia Fatima, the fourth daughter was born on 25th November 1927. She was adopted by the elder brother of Deen Yar Jung, Mohiuddin Ahmed, and was educated at the Mahboobia Girls' School. She was married to Mahmood Ali, an Industrialist on 9th March 1950.

Mahmood Ali was son of Nawab Ehtesham-ud-Daula of Madras.

They have two daughters, Fawzia and Daisy.

Fawzia is married to Naseer Ansari, an Architech and they have three children, Faiz, Faraaz, and Farah Naaz.

Daisy is married to Mohammed Azher Siddiqui and they have two children, Raza and Laila.

Ruqhia M. Ali's 'Bismillah' at Aziz Bagh, 1932.

Deen Yar Jung with his twelve grandchildren:

Cousins 1951

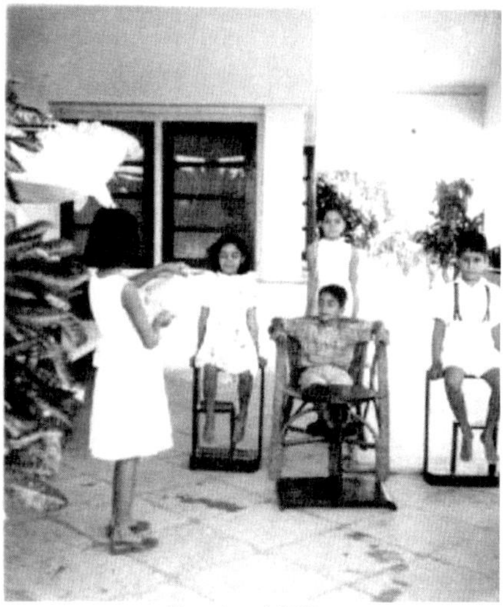

Cousins 1958

Cousins 17th June 1959 - Masood Hyder, Nisar Hyder, Abbas Hussain, Rizwana Farooq, Shamsuddin Ahmed, Daisy Siddiqui, Zaheer Ahmed, Fawzia Ansari, Mohammed Azher Siddiqui, Nasreen Ahmed, Mariam Farooq and Farhana Zia..

Ruknuddin Ahmed

b 1900 – d 1993

Ruknuddin Ahmed was the fourth son of Nawab Aziz Jung.

After graduating from college, Ruknuddin Ahmed went to Bombay for training in finance. Upon completion of the training he was appointed as Treasure Officer at Gulbarga. He was then promoted as Assistant Accountant General, and worked his way up to become Deputy Accountant General at Hyderabad and later served the Indian Railways as Financial Advisor. He was also Secretary to Government PWD (Power Works Department). He retired as Senior Deputy Accountant General. After the Indian Independence he accepted the position of Accountant General at H.E.H. the Nizam's Private Estate.

During his service and after the retirement Ruknuddin Ahmed continued public activities. He served as a Member and Chairman of the Board at various colleges.

He married Aziz Fatima, daughter of Nawab Mabood Nawaz Jung. Like his older brother Mohiuddin Ahmed, he was also known for his exceptional sense of humor and lovely personality. He will be remembered for generations.

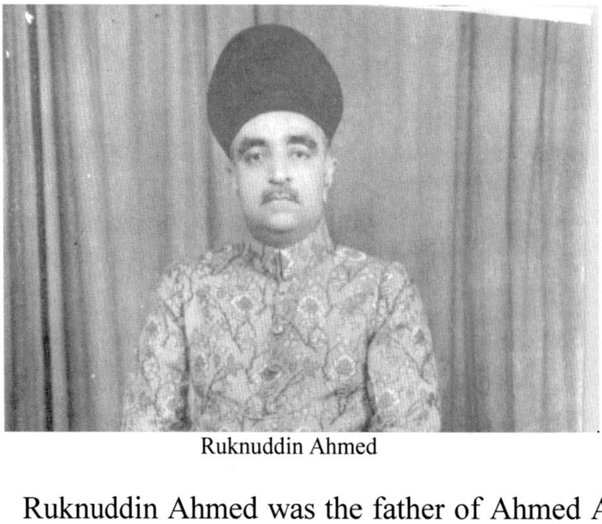

Ruknuddin Ahmed

Aziz Fatima

Ruknuddin Ahmed was the father of Ahmed Abdul Aziz Asif, Hafeez Kamran, Anees H. Ahmed and Jahanara Hussain.

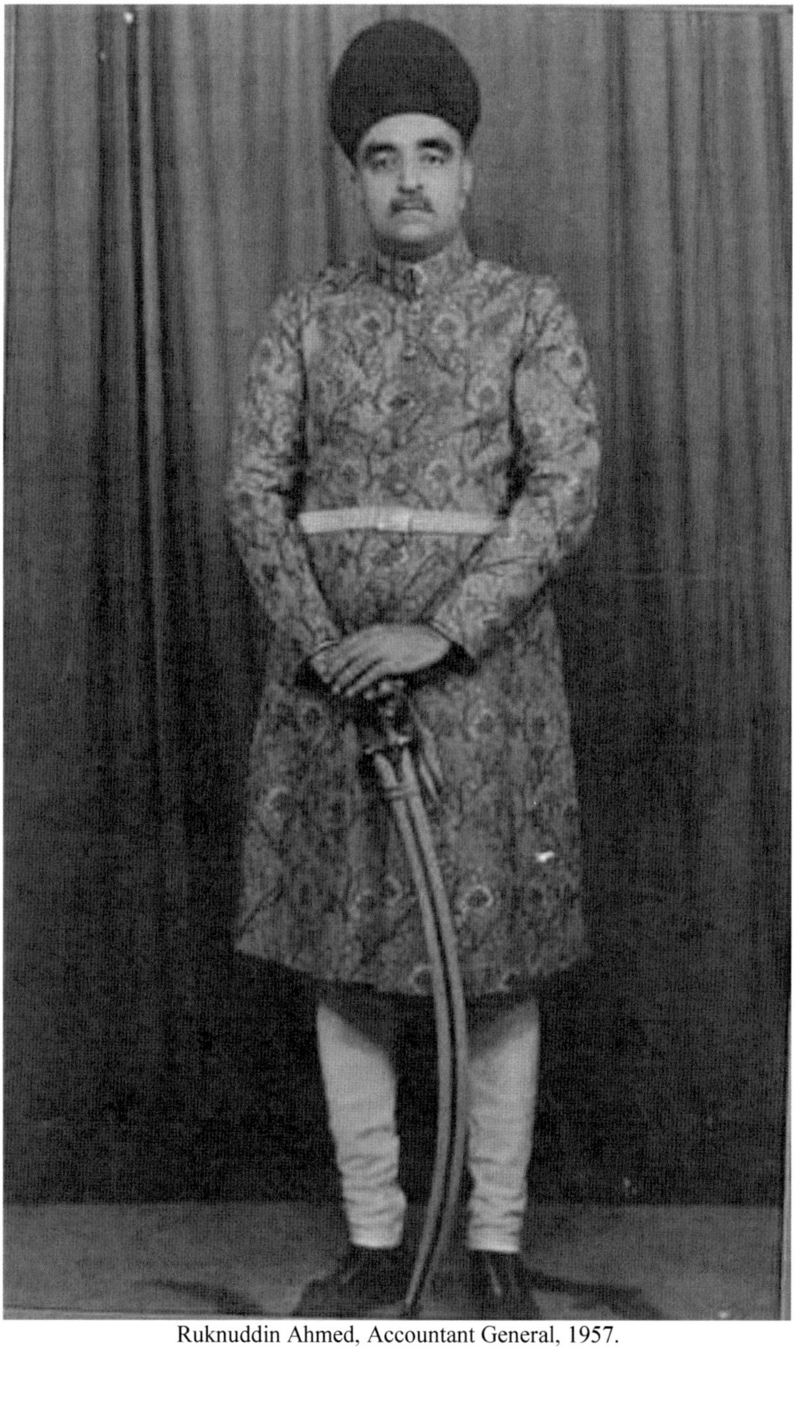

Ruknuddin Ahmed, Accountant General, 1957.

He was an ardent chess player, whose chess partner was none other than his challenger, and favorite cousin and brother-in-law, Mohammed Valiullah. These two chess players were a great source of entertainment for the family. Their humorous remarks to each other were very entertaining for the spectators, both young and old.

He was an honest, loving and kind person, with a very sharp memory. He was an ocean of knowledge. He remembered nearly every incident of his life and was a great resource to others.

He was a very detailed narrator of stories. His delivery was both humorous and theatrical. It was as if you were there when that incident actually happened. He made the story very interesting for the listener.

His greatest characteristic was that he despised retaliation. His behavior towards even his adversaries and opponents was one of gentle and exemplary tolerance. His favorite slogans were; "live and let live", "forgive and forget", "give and take".

Ruknuddin Ahmed and Aziz Fatima with their children and grand children, 1966.
Seated L. to R: Anees H. Ahmed, Soghra Aziz, Ruknuddin Ahmed, Aziz Fatima, Shameem Kamran, and Jahanara Hussain.
Standing L. to R: Dr. Hasanuddin Ahmed, Ahmed Abdul Aziz (Asif), Shamsuddin Ahmed, Shahana Hyder, Zaheer Ahmed, Hafeez Kamran, and Mohammed Hussain.
Seated on carpet L. to R: Nida Mohiuddin, Romana Sayeed, and Nahid Fatima Khan

Ruknuddin Ahmed had an excellent taste for food and expected only quality where food was concerned. If someone invited him for dinner, the hosts would hold their breaths until he made a positive comment. Ruknuddin Ahmed always made a comment after eating good food, and always complimented the cook and the host promptly.

Ruknuddin Ahmed and his children, grand children and great-grand children, 1982.

Ruknuddin Ahmed's residence, within the Aziz Bagh compound, 1982.

Ruknuddin Ahmed with his brother Deen Yar Jung, 1946.

Ruknuddin Ahmed was a brilliant mathematician who could calculate complex equations effortlessly, without the use of a calculator. Calculators were not invented until he was well into his late fifties.

When he was sick and his diet was regulated, he was very displeased. When the family physician Dr. Mannan heard about his unhappiness, he remarked, “let Ruknuddin Ahmed eat anything, food will never harm him”.

A happy and cheerful person often lives long, it was true for Ruknuddin Ahmed, who lived 93 memorable years, and still lives in everyone’s hearts.

Ruknuddin Ahmed's sons and daughters

Major Ahmed Abdul Aziz (Asif), first child of Ruknuddin Ahmed was, born on 24th July 1927. He served the Hyderabad Army as Major, and Staff Officer of H.E. H. the Nizam VII of Hyderabad.

Ahmed Abdul Aziz, (Asif), 1999.

He is currently a Wildlife Conservation activist, Honorary Wildlife Warden Government of Andhra Pradesh.

Wildlife Conservation Activities:
Aziz Bagh members are very environment conscious, and care for the wellbeing of not only human beings but about birds and animals. Ahmed Abdul Aziz is a very dedicated wildlife activist.

He is a Life Member Bird Watcher's Society of Andhra Pradesh, member Society for nature conservation. He is a subscriber Benefactor Worldwide Fund for Nature - India. Among other activities, he is also a Life member - Friends of Trees, Kerala, India. Ahmed Abdul Aziz is a Life member - Bombay Natural History Society, Life member - Society for Environmental Education, Kerala, India, Life member -

Wildlife Preservation Society of India, member - World Pheasant Association, India.

He is a member Fauna and Flora Preservation Society of London, Associate Member national Wildlife Federation, U.S.A. Member National Wildlife Action Plan Working Group Voluntary Bodies, Government of India, Honorary member Massachusetts Audubon Society, U.S.A.

He is also a member Society for Preservation of Environment and Quality of Life, Hyderabad, Life member Zoo outreach Organization Coimbatore, Tamil Nadu, India. Member Conservation Breeding Special Group, India. Member Nilgiri Wildlife and Environment Association, the Nilgiris, Uthagamandalam, Tamil Nadu, India. Member Salim Ali Centre for Ornithology and Natural History (SACON) and the list goes on and on.

Ahmed Abdul Aziz is married to Soghra Fatima. They have two daughters, Nida Fatima, married to Sultan Mohiuddin. Sultan is an IT professional. Nida has two children, Imran and Yasmeen.

Nahid Fatima, married to Sharfuddin Khan.

Left Picture: Nahid and Nida
Right Picture: Ahmed Abdul Aziz's family Portrait, with Soghra, Nida, Sultan Mohiuddin, Imran, Yasmeen, Nahid and Sharfuddin Khan (Sadath).

Hafeez Kamran, the second child of Ruknuddin Ahmed was born on 27th July 1928 in Hyderabad. Initially his father Ruknuddin Ahmed named him Ahmed Abdul Hafeez. He migrated to Pakistan at a very young age. When Hafeez migrated to Pakistan he changed the name to Hafeez Kamran. He was a very hard working and a self-made man.

His early life as a new immigrant to a newly established country Pakistan was very tough. He struggled for many years, but his hard work and dedicated efforts resulted in a very lucrative future for him. He was a Regional Manager TWA (Trans World Airlines) for Pakistan and Afghanistan. Later he was Chief Operations Manager for Saudi Airlines.

He married to Shameem Dost Ali Khan, an educator. Shameem belongs to a well known Hyderabadi family. Shameem is an English teacher. She teaches at a reputable college in the Chicago area. They have two sons, Imad Kamran and Faraaz Kamran.

Hafeez Kamran 1976.

Hafeez Kamran passed away at a very young age of 50 years on 26th February 1978.

Imad Kamran, Director, Global Technology Group, Merrill Lynch. Imad married to Linda and they have one son, Adam Hafeez Kamran.

Faraaz Kamran, Director, Healthcare Leveraged Finance, Madison Capital Funding. Faraaz married to Sayeda Reema and they have triplets; Suleiman Abdul Hafeez Kamran, Ibrahim Abd-Allah Kamran, and Eisa Abdur-Rahman Kamran.

Imad Kamran and Faraaz Kamran
at their great grandfather's house Aziz Bagh.

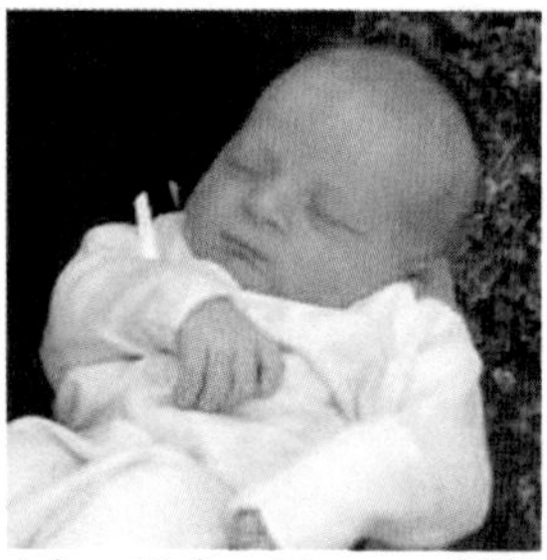

Adam Hafeez Kamran, 2009

Ibrahim, Eisa and Suleiman, 2008

Anees H. Ahmed, wife of Dr. Hasanuddin Ahmed.

Anees H. Ahmed is the third child of Ruknuddin Ahmed. She is married to Hasanuddin Ahmed. They have two sons Shamsuddin Ahmed, married to Farzana daughter of Mohammed Ahmedullah.

Zaheer Ahmed married to Razia daughter of Syed Valiullah Bukhari, Editor Milap daily newspaper.

Shamsuddin Ahmed has four daughters:
Fatima is married to Aqeel Abbas.
Sameha is married to Syed Ahsanullah Hussaini Saberi, and they have four children, Arman, Aiman, Adnan and Hanan.
Faria is married to Syed Hamid Hussaini Saberi (Hamid), they have three children, Ryan, Zoya and Zaid.
Naila is a college student.

Shamsuddin Ahmed's youngest daughter Naila with her nephews and nieces, 2007.
Left to Right: Ryan, Aiman, Adnan, Arman, and Zoya.

Arman

Aiman

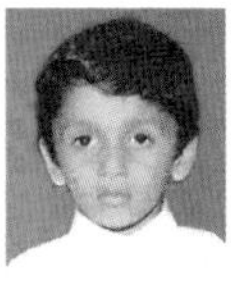

Adnan

Riyan

Zoya

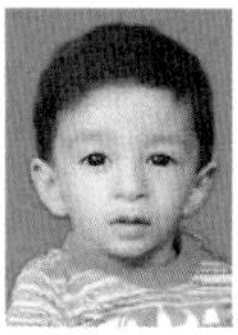

Zaid

Zaheer's children: Hana is married to Syed Mansoor Ali Khan, J.D. an Attorney-at-Law, Estate Planning and son of Syed Mohammed Ali Khan and Sayeda Zuhoor Khan. Zaheer's youngest daughter is Saba. Saba is engaged to be married to Sameer Aleem, a Law student, son of Mohammed Aleem and Sadequa Aleem.

Zaheer and Razia Ahmed with Hana and Saba.

Hana and Mansoor Khan

Jahanara Hussain is the fourth child of Ruknuddin Ahmed. She was married to Mohammed Hussain, an Industrialist. Mohammed Hussain was son of Nawab Ehtesham-ud-Daula of Madras.

They have two daughters:
Shahana married to Masood Hyder who works for the United Nations' World Food Program. Shahana's children: Sana, Mohammed, and Nashuan.

Romana, married to Jaweed Sayeed, Computer Systems Analyst. Jaweed is the grandson of Dr. Lateef Sayeed, an eminent physician and a devoted nationalist. Romana's children: Ayesha, Sayyada, and Hussain.

Picture taken in London, UK in 1972.
Dr. Hasanuddin Ahmed, Anees H. Ahmed, Jahanara Hussain and Mohammed Hussain.

Jahanara Hussain with the President of I ndia A.P.J. Abul Kalam.

Chapter 6

The Aziz Bagh Album

Aziz Bagh was built over one century ago. The family of Aziz Jung is represented by very highly cultured, educated, simple and professional individuals. They are hard working sincere and they display loyalty to their superiors.

A picture is worth a thousand words. It refers to the idea that long stories can be described with just a single snap-shot image, or that an image may be more revealing than a substantial length of text. A picture tells a story. This album is an attempt to sum up Aziz Bagh's heritage in a nutshell.

The House of Aziz Jung may not be situated in the best of Geographical locations, but Aziz Bagh has a lot of history.

The very rare album that follows will display such historical events that may have been forgotten otherwise over time. The purpose of this book is to revive and display awareness of the glory of Aziz Bagh.

Every resident of Aziz Bagh, who is a descendent of Aziz Jung, although scattered globally, are all well placed in their own territory and maintain the cultural background that they inherited from their forefathers.

The family unity of the Aziz Jung's descendants is well known. The family traditional values are not forgotten. The family unity can be witnessed when one visits Aziz Bagh with individual residential extensions. The traditional family cooking, the importance of education, and the importance of self respect are very clearly visible.

Aziz Bagh, the Heritage of Culture

Aziz Bagh, close-up.

The Photo Album Contents

Aziz Jung Rare Pictures

Rare picture of Aziz Jung with dignitaries of Hyderabad Deccan, 1922.

Deen Yar Jung as a Child

Moulvi Nizamuddin Ahmed (left) and his brother Ruknuddin Ahmed, and Nizamuddin Ahmed's three grandchildren, Ghazi Yar Jung, Mohiuddin Ahmed and Deen Yar Jung. 1897

Deen Yar Jung was born on Tuesday 26th September 1893 at Hyderabad in a house across from Aziz Bagh, before Aziz Bagh was built. He was six years old when he moved to the newly constructed Aziz Bagh in 1899.

This little 4 year old boy grew up to be one of the most famous persons in Hyderabad Deccan.

He received first ten years of education at home. When he was ten years old, he was admitted to the 'Aaizza' Elementary school, which was famous for its educational excellence.

He received his high school education at Aliya High School, which was also one of the most competitive schools in the state at the time.

Left, Deen Yar Jung as a child. Right, Deen Yar Jung at age 4 years 4 months, ready for his 'Bismillah'.

While at college he developed the requisite talent needed to enter public life. After passing his Matriculation exam from the Madras-Bombay College with high honors, he graduated from the Nizam College. The level of education in those days was extremely high teachers took a personal interest in the studies of their students.

Deen Yar Jung and his Family

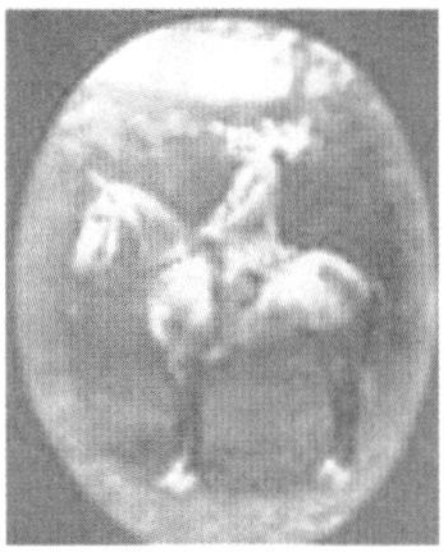

While working as the District Revenue Officer at Osmanabad District, Deen Yar Jung married Fatima Begum on 11th April 1919. Aziz Fatima was the daughter of Dr. Fakhiuddin Hussain, a Civil Surgeon of Khurshid Jahi Paigah.

Dr. Fakhiuddin Hussain,
Deen Yar Jung's father-in-law
He was a surgeon Khurshid Jahi Paiga.

Dr. Fakhiuddin Hussain was a descendent of the Royal Wallajahi Family of Arcot. He was son of Khairuddin Khan Mahmood Jung, Judge of the High Court Hyderabad, and grandson of the well known scholar and reformer, Khan-e-Alam Khan (Tahwar Jung), who was the grandson of Mohammed Ali Khan Wallajahi's sister.

Dr. Fakhiuddin Hussain was himself a great scholar, poet and linguist and was fluent in seven languages.

Fatima Begum was born on 5th November 1902. She received her early education at home and was fluent in several languages like her father.

Fatima Begum Deen Yar Jung and her children.

Deen Yar Jung and his wife Fatima Begum, 1943.

Deen Yar Jung's children, in 1941,
Aziz Ahmed, Soghra, Zehra, Razia, Ruqhia, Hasanuddin Ahmed.

Deen Yar Jung's Children Sixty years later in 2001.

Hasanuddin Ahmed and Aziz Ahmed 2004.

Deen Yar Jung with his sons.

Deen Yar Jung with his two sons, Hasanuddin Ahmed and Aziz Ahmed.

Left, Deen Yar Jung with his two sons. Right, with his sons and grandsons.

Deen Yar Jung and Ruknuddin Ahmed's Daughters:

L. to R: Jahanara Hussain, Soghra Khan , Razia Siddiqui, Zehra Hyder, Anees. H. Ahmed and Ruqhia M. Ali.

Sitting L. to R: Razia Siddiqui, Anees H. Ahmed, Zehra Hyder.
Standing L. to R: Soghra Khan and Ruqhia M. Ali.

Ruqhia's Bismillah. Aziz Jung's grand children, 1931.

Ruqhia's Bismillah.
Mohiuddin Ahmed with his favorite niece Ruqia, 1931.

Deen Yar Jung as DGP, Director General Police

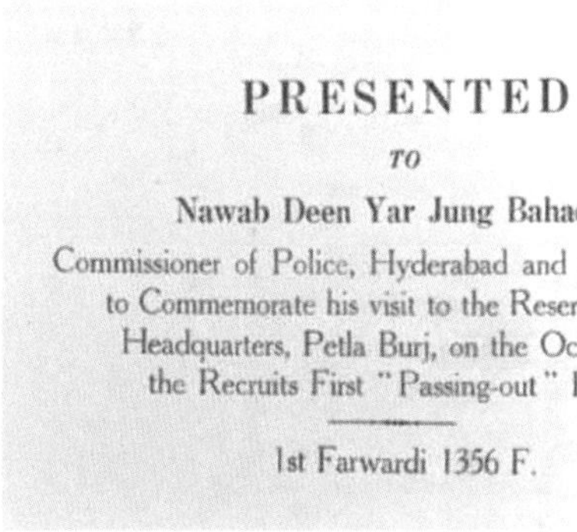
PRESENTED

TO

Nawab Deen Yar Jung Bahadur,

Commissioner of Police, Hyderabad and Secunderabad, to Commemorate his visit to the Reserve Police, Headquarters, Petla Burj, on the Occasion of the Recruits First "Passing-out" Parade

1st Farwardi 1356 F.

Deen Yar Jung as Director General Police.

Police Training:

Deen Yar Jung was sent to Bombay for practical police training. After completing the training, he returned to Hyderabad, where on 6th June 1944 he succeeded Rahmat Yar Jung as Commissioner of Police.

Deen Yar Jung with Sir Mirza Ismail and Sir Mohammed Zafarullah Khan at Aziz Bagh along with high ranking Police Officials on 22nd January 1945.

At the Police Headquarters, Hyderabad, 1947.

During a routine inspection.

Soon after he took charge as Police Commissioner, a celebration was held by the Police Department in his honor as a new Chief.

Within two years, Deen Yar Jung completely overhauled the Hyderabad Police Department and restored its reputation as protector of the citizens.

Deen Yar Jung inspecting an Army tank.

Deen Yar Jung inspecting the guards.

Deen Yar Jung was soon promoted to the highest Police position, in the police force, Director General of Police on 31st July 1947. Deen Yar Jung's promotion was a result of his exceptional abilities as an administrator.

During the Police officers' football game.

Deen Yar Jung's promotion to the highest police position was welcomed by all citizens in the state. He was regarded as an ardent public servant and well-wisher of both the State and its Ruler, the Nizam.

H.E.H. the Nizam expressed his praise for the exceptional services performed by Deen Yar Jung both as Commissioner of City Police and as Director General of Police.

Deen Yar Jung served as the Commissioner of City Police
and Director General Police until 1947.

Deen Yar Jung took charge as Director General Police at the worst of times. The Indian Government was struggling for Independence from the British, while the Ruler of Hyderabad State, H.E.H. the Nizam struggled to keep his State from being taken over by the Indian Government.

Law and order was at its worst, and Deen Yar Jung had to tackle this delicate situation diplomatically without stirring agitation among the common citizens while at the same time maintaining trust with the Ruler of State.

In an editorial in the 2nd August 1947 issue of The Subhe Deccan entitled, “A Fitting Selection”, the newspaper praised Deen Yar Jung’s selection as Director General of Police.

Deen Yar Jung with World Dignitaries

Deen Yar Jung and Nizam VII, the Ruler of Hyderabad Deccan, 1943.

Deen Yar Jung with the first President of India, Dr. Rajendra Prashad, 1951.

Deen Yar Jung with Nizam VII the Ruler of Hyderabad Deccan.

Left to Right: Ali Pasha, Nizam's son-in-law, Deen Yar Jung, Nizam VII, and Moazam Jah, second son of Nizam VII.

Police Headquarters Opening Ceremony. Left to Right: Hosh Yar Jung, Dost Mohammed Allauddin, Nizam VII, Deen Yar Jung and Mirza Humayun Ali Baig.

Nizam VII, Deen Yar Jung, Hosh Yar Jung at Police Headquarters.

After Indian Independence, H.E.H. the Nizam offered Deen Yar Jung yet another very important position, Chairman of the Nizam's private estate on 1st January 1955.

Deen Yar Jung at the Royal Group Portrait with H.E.H. the Nizam VII, the Ruler of Hyderabad Deccan, and the Royal Family.

Deen Yar Jung with the Nizam VII, Rajendra Prashad, President of India, Ali Pasha and other members of the royal family, 1951.

Deen Yar Jung was Chairman of the newly set up Managing Committee. He set up a special staff to execute work expeditiously and with no days off, not even holidays. In order to eliminate all possible delays he provided the staff with a manual of procedures and guidelines.

Deen Yar Jung extreme right.

Deen Yar Jung at the Police camp during Nizam's inspection.

Besides enjoying the confidence of H.E.H the Nizam, he was also an advisor to the Royal Family who on occasion asked for his guidance and advice on various administrative matters.

During Deen Yar Jung's illness, when he underwent surgery, the Nizam personally called and confirmed his well being, and sanctioned his hospital and medical expenses. He was granted a 3 month leave of absence.

Left Picture: Deen Yar Jung, Mohammed Hyder, Nisar Hyder, Ruknuddin Ahmed, Governor Bhimsen Sachar, Dr. Hasanuddin Ahmed, and Masood Hyder, 1956.
Right picture: Deen Yar Jung with the President of India, Dr. Rajendra Prashad, 1951.

Deen Yar Jung in front of Aziz Bagh. Also seen in the picture, Zehra Hyder, daughter of Deen Yar Jung, Mohammed Hyder, Ruknuddin Ahmed, Sir. Arthur Lothian, Nasreen and Farhana. Nasreen and Farhana, are two of Deen Yar Jung's granddaughters.

Sayedana Sabed Past and Present

Left picture: Deen Yar Jung with Sayedna Saheb head of Bhora community.
Right picture: Deen Yar Jung with his best friend, Nawab Khudrat Nawaz Jung.

Left picture; Deen Yar Jung and Dr. Hasanuddin Ahmed during Prime Minister Jawaharlal Nehru's visit to Hyderabad. Right picture; Deen Yar Jung with Governor Bhimsen Sachar, 1962.

Deen Yar Jung with Nizam VII at an inspection of the Police Camp.

L to R: Ruknuddin Ahmed, Basheer Ahmed Tahir, I.A.S., and Deen Yar Jung.

Very rare portrait. Left to Right sitting; Mohammed Hyder, Hasanuddin Ahmed, Ahmed Abdul Aziz Asif, unidentified, unidentified, Deen Yar Jung, unidentified, unidentified, Aziz Ahmed, Ruknuddin Ahmed and Mohammed Ahmedullah.

Wedding of Mohammed Hyder

The wedding of Mohammed Hyder, Deen Yar Jung's first son-in-law to Zehra. Nizam VII attended the wedding at Aziz Bagh.
First row: Mohiuddin Ahmed, Ghazi Yar Jung, Ahmed Abdul Aziz (Asif), Nizam VII, Mohammed Hyder, Deen Yar Jung, Aziz Ahmed and Yousufuddin Ahmed.
In the row behind: Mohammed Habibullah, Ruknuddin Ahmed, Mohammed Valiullah, Yusuf Hussain and Mohammed Asadullah.
1st May 1942.

Masood Hyder

Nisar Hyder

Rizwana Hyder

Nizam VII attended Mohammed Hyder's Wedding

Nizam VII, Ruler of Hyderabad, Mohammed Hyder, and Deen Yar Jung, 1942.

Mohammed Hyder.

Wedding of Ahmeduddin Siddiqui – 1

The wedding of Ahmeduddin Siddiqui, Deen Yar Jung's second son-in-law to Razia on 23rd November, 1945.
Standing on left: Yousufuddin Ahmed, Ruknuddin Ahmed, Mohammed Ahmedullah, Hasanuddin Ahmed, Mohammed Hyder, and Aziz Ahmed.
Sitting from left to right: Sir Arthur Lothian and Nawab of Chhatari.

Wedding of Ahmeduddin Siddiqui – 2

The wedding of Ahmeduddin Siddiqui, Deen Yar Jung's second son-in-law to Razia on 23rd November, 1945.
Some people identified in this picture: Deen Yar Jung's uncle Abdul Azeez Chida, Asad Ali, Deen Yar Jung's brother-in-law Mohiuddin,
and Mahant Baba Purandas (sitting on extreme right in a black robe and beard).
Also in the picture are Sir Arthur Lothian and Nawab of Chhatari.

Wedding of Ahmed Hussain Khan

The wedding of Ahmed Hussain Khan Deen Yar Jung's third son-in-law to Soghra on 30th November 1945.

Picture taken during Nabil Farooq's wdding, Hyderabad, January 2001.

Wedding of Dr. Hasanuddin Ahmed

Dr. Hasanuddin Ahmed's wedding, 1st May 1947
Sir Nizamath Jung may be seen along with the Aziz Bagh family members.

Wedding portrait of Dr. Hasanuddin Ahmed and Anees H. Ahmed, 1st May 1947.

Family portrait on the occasion of Dr. Hasanuddin Ahmed's wedding.

Dr. Hasanuddin Ahmed with his family, Anees H. Ahmed, Shamsuddin Ahmed and Zaheer Ahmed, 1954.

Wedding of Mahmood Ali

The wedding of Mahmood Ali Deen Yar Jung's fourth son-in-law to Ruqhia on 9th March1950.

Fawzia and Naseer Ansari.

Left to Right: Laila, Daisy, Mohammed Azher Siddiqui, Raza, Faiz, Farah and Faraz.

Wedding of Shamsuddin Ahmed

Wedding of Shamsuddin Ahmed, great-grandson of Aziz Jung in 1975.

Dr. Hasanuddin Ahmed in Japan 1954 World Religion Conference

World Religion Congress conference in Japan 1954.

Dr. Hasanuddin Ahmed, Mrs. Anees H. Ahmed and the foreign delegates at the World Religion Congress Conference in Japan 1954.

世界宗教會議

Dr. Hasanuddin Ahmed with Dignitaries

Dr. Hasanuddin Ahmed and Anees H. Ahmed with Prime Minister of India Indira Gandhi during the 1973 book release of 'Word Count'.

Dr. Hasanuddin Ahmed presenting the book to Prime Minister Indira Gandhi. Information and Broadcasting Minister I. K. Gujral in on the right. Ahmed Abdul Aziz (Asif) may be seen on extreme right.

Prime Minister Indira Gandhi praising the book during the release ceremony.

Left to right: Anees H. Ahmed, Mrs. Hasanuddin Ahmed, and Prime Minister Indira Gandhi.

Dr. Hasanuddin Ahmed and Anees H. Ahmed with President of India Fakhruddin Ali Ahmed and First Lady during the release of another book authored by Hasanuddin Ahmed.

Left to Right; Shamsuddin Ahmed, Ahmed Abdul Aziz Asif, Dr. Hasanuddin Ahmed, and Governor Surjit Singh Barnala during a book release ceremony in Hyderabad.

Dr. Hasanuddin Ahmed with Governor Surjit Singh Barnala on another book release in Chennai.

From left: Fatima, Ahmed Abdul Aziz Asif, Anees H. Ahmed, Jahanara Hussain, unidentified, Dr. Hasanuddin Ahmed, and Governor Surgit Singh Barnala.

Dr. Hasanuddin Ahmed I.A.S. (Right) with Hashim Ali Akhter I.A.S, former Vice Chancellor of Osmania University and Aligarh Muslim University.

Dr. Hasanuddin Ahmed in Iran

Famous Aziz Bagh Badam-ki-Jali, Ashrafi and Various Fruits and Designs

Tasty and colorful delights prepared by none other than Farzana Ahmed. These Aziz Bagh specialties are prepared one at a time. The famous 'Badam-ki-Jali', 'Ashrafi', and fruit shaped desserts taste even better than they look in the pictures.

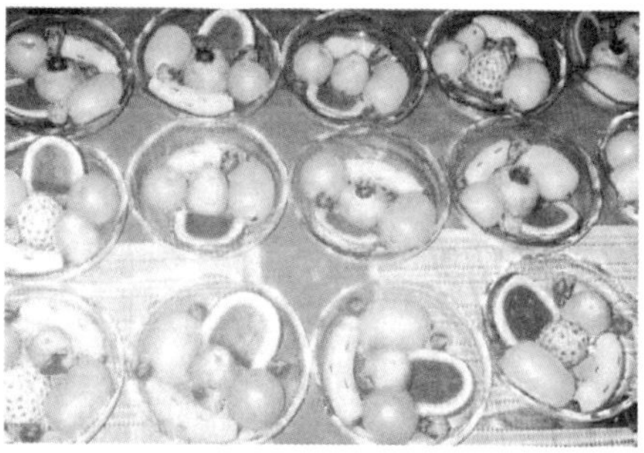

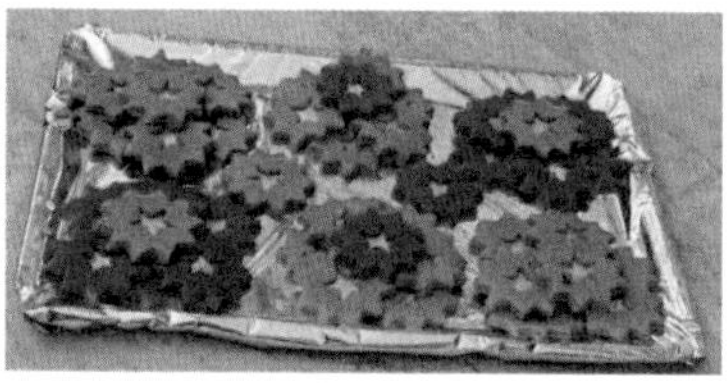

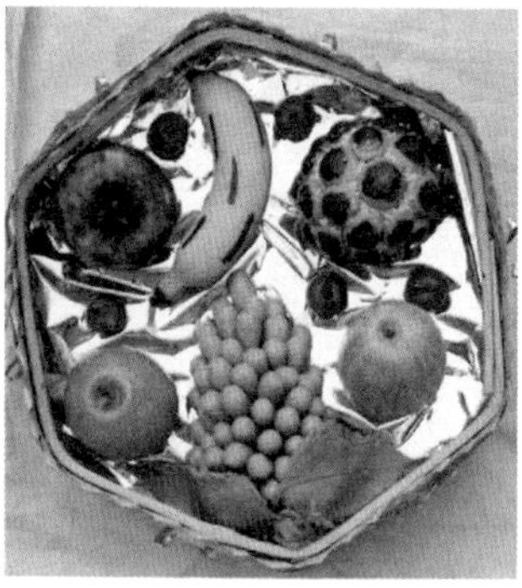

'Badam-ki-Jali', with its combination of almonds and sugar, has been a traditional desert for centuries' in the Aziz Bagh family. Besides the

“Badam-ki-Jali, ‘Ashrafis’ (Gold Coin) replicas, fruit designs are also Aziz Bagh family traditional desserts.. These marvels are created out of a very simple but elegant recipe of Almonds and sugar, and the resulting 'dough' is quite flexible. Expert family members use this element to create fanciful figures.

These trays, prepared one at a time, and with the utmost care, are the favorite delights to many. These party delights are admired by everyone that tastes them.

The Jalis and Ashrafis derive its characteristic flavor from almonds and sugar in a specific ratio. Saffron is added to create a unique and elegant flavor. Various food colors and rose water are sometimes added to create a specific taste and effect.

They are traditionally made for special occasions, such as weddings, and birthdays. They are shaped into practically anything imaginable.

The recipe originally came from the Middle-East, and it was known as 'lozina', which is derived from the word, 'لوز' *(lawz)*, the Arabic word for almonds.

Inside Aziz Bagh

Elegant front view of Aziz Bagh.

Beautiful summer retreat.

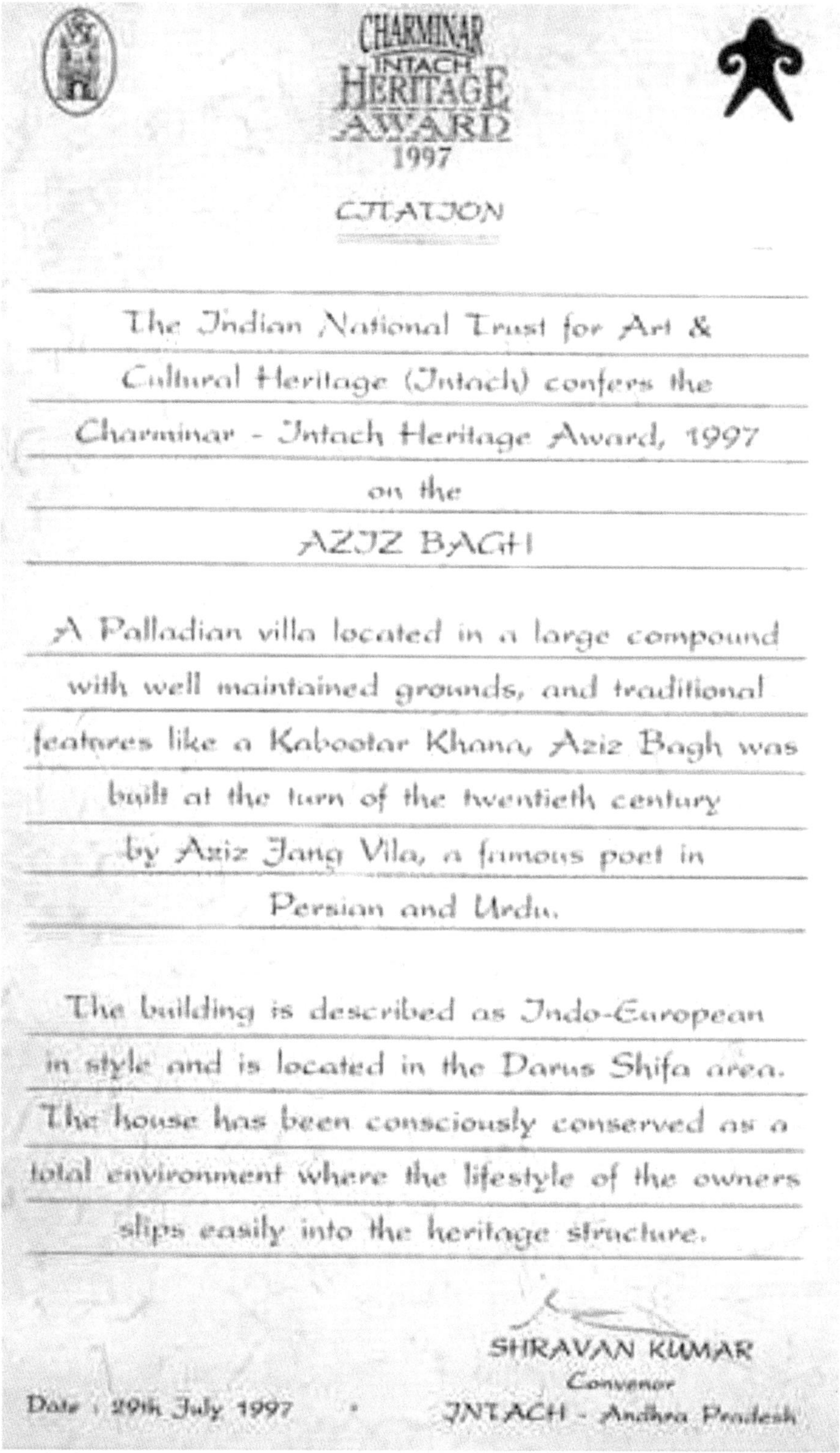

CHARMINAR INTACH HERITAGE AWARD 1997

CITATION

The Indian National Trust for Art & Cultural Heritage (Intach) confers the Charminar - Intach Heritage Award, 1997 on the

AZIZ BAGH

A Palladian villa located in a large compound with well maintained grounds, and traditional features like a Kabootar Khana, Aziz Bagh was built at the turn of the twentieth century by Aziz Jang Vila, a famous poet in Persian and Urdu.

The building is described as Indo-European in style and is located in the Darus Shifa area. The house has been consciously conserved as a total environment where the lifestyle of the owners slips easily into the heritage structure.

SHRAVAN KUMAR
Convenor
INTACH - Andhra Pradesh

Date : 29th July 1997

The heritage award certificate INTACH (The India National Trust for Arts and Cultural Heritage) was given to Aziz Bagh on 29th July 2007.

Dr. Hasanuddin Ahmed in the front veranda.

A relaxing moment in the veranda, just as the day begins. Here Dr. Ahmed waits for the morning news paper. An early riser, he works diligently throughout the day.

For the dwellers of this house, the atmosphere of the surroundings is more important than the mere beauty of the structure itself.

Aziz Bagh is identified with the magnificent culture of Hyderabad. It is a residence of people who are very talented and highly educated. This house is not a mere haven for its residents, but it is a heritage, 'A Heritage of Culture'.

Hasanuddin Ahmed in the front veranda.

During the course of the day, Dr. Hasanuddin Ahmed frequently returns to the veranda meet people, interview students, and to listen to any-one that needs his advice.

Marvelous view through the veranda.

View of the front entrance of Aziz Bagh.

The members of the Aziz Jung family take enormous pride in their ancestral home, and they have every reason. This place has witnessed history in the making, including charitable contributions to the needy; and literary events.

Many dignitaries visited and admired not only its beauty, but the Residents as well, who are not only humble, but also very down-to-earth. The descendents of Aziz Jung are modest, yet very highly qualified in their own profession.

The Aziz Bagh Drawing Room

The Drawing Room of Aziz Bagh is occupied by historical portraits of eminent family members, as well as portraits of Royal Family members of the time.

Overlooking the drawing room is Aziz Jung's library of books that he authored. During his lifetime, Aziz Jung authored 29 books on various subjects such as agriculture (cultivation of grapes), history, law, and literature to name a few. He was a well known Persian and Urdu poet and scholar.

In 1900 a printing press was located at Aziz Bagh. Most of Aziz Jung's books were published there, and a journal called 'Aziz-ul-Akhbar' was also published from this press.

Dr. Hasanuddin Ahmed also authored several books, at Aziz Bagh that are acclaimed worldwide. The family tradition of literary talent still continues till this day.

Antique china is stored in 18th Century Gothic Style in the kitchen.

Aziz Jung Library of books that Aziz Jung authored.

Just behind this gorgeous library of books authored by members of the family, is the awesome dining room.

Partially visible dining room.

Dinning room in sunlight.

Marvelous cut-glass hurricane lantern stands in front of the stained-glass windows in the dining room.

'L' shaped veranda where Deen Yar Jung used to sit, read and write.

Chapter 7

Daughters of Aziz Jung

Azizunissa Begum was the first daughter of Aziz Jung. She was married to Yakhub Hasan Jaddi. From Azizunissa Begum's first marriage to Yakhub they had one daughter Zehra Begum (Shahzadi Begum), and one son Zainulabdin Ahmed Bashir.

Azizunisa Begum in Aziz Bagh Drawing Room.
This chair is still in the drawing room today.

Zainulabedin Ahmed, Basheer was an athletic and a great tennis player. He won several trophies. He passed away at an early age of 28 years.

Zehra Begum was married to Gulam Fakhruddin and they had seven sons and four daughters. Gulam Fakhruddin was a Magistrate at the Nalgunda District. After retirement from Government service, he accepted an assignment of higher position in Zaheer Yar Jung's Paigah as Awwal Talaquadar at Chatguppa. He worked on this position for a substantial period of time.

Zehra Begum (Shahzadi Begum)

Magistrate Gulam Fakhruddin

Zehra Begum's seven sons were **Hameduddin Fazil, Azizuddin Afzal, Fasiuddin, Viquaruddin, Habeenuddin Sabir, Zainulabedeen Shakir, Iftekharuddin Shameem, and her four daughters were Soghra, Razia, Aziza and Safia.**

Family picture of children and grand children of Magistrate Gulam Fakhruddin and Zehra Begum Taken in Hyderabad, at ZFWS (Zehra Family Welfare Society) Milan 2006.

Yakhub Hasan Jaddi passed away and Azizunissa Begum was widowed at a young age. Upon insistence of her father Aziz Jung, she was remarried to Mohammed Hussain Makki. Makki was born in Madras and later settled in Hyderabad. He worked for Aziz Jung and was in charge of book binding section in Azizal Mutabey at Aziz Bagh.

Azizunisa Begum had one son Nazir and six daughters from her second marriage to Makki.

Yousufuddin Makki, Nazir and his sister Ismatunisa Begum

Yusufuddin Makki's children: Shaheen, Parveen,, Nasreen, Shereen, Moseen, Taseen and Zaheer (Haseen). Shereen's children: Taha, Wajahat, Tehyniyat Zaheer (Haseen)'s children: Sufian, Yousuf, Vajeeh, Azeem.

1 - Zainab Begum
Her Children: Samdani, Shahzamani, Fareed Abdul Rahman Raheem, Khaleelur Rahman, Habibur Rahman Muneer, Anwer and Sarwar.

2 - Ismathunissa Begum, (Manjli Begum)
Her children: Akbar, Anwar, Azhar, Iqbal, Akhter, Afsar and Ashraff.

Ashraf (Nikhat) married Naim Abbas, and they have one son Hashim and one daughter Nazia. Hashim has three daughters, Afra, Afia and Alia.

Nazia married Dr. Nasser Omar Qadri, Neuclear Radiologist, and they have one son Nawaz and one daughter Nailyah.

3 – Ghousia Begum, (Chunnu Begum)
Her children: Mohammed Badrul Islam (Haji), Dr. Yakhut Badrul Islam (Noorjehan), and Dr. Badrul Islam (Abida). Haji's daughter Sameena Badar Jahan is B.Sc, MLT and works at Azam Junior Vocational College. Dr. Badrul Islam is married to Mirza Osman Baig and they have six children. Lubna is married to Karamat Ali, Mirza Irfan Baig is married to Syeda Asma, Reshma is married to Mohammed Asif, Arshia is married to Mohammed Abdul Majid, Urusa is married to Ali Mohammed Nizamuddin, and Mahelaqua is married to Amanullah Nizamuddin.

4 - Ahmedi Begum
Her children: Syeda, Sajida Sabhia, Mahmood Hussain, Rayeesa, Shameem, and Fareeda Shahida.

5 - Mahmooda Begum
Mahmooda Begum had 5 children:
Naseem Abbas, Nafees Viqar, Mohammed Ather Abbas, Najma Siqddiqui, and Dr. Azher Abbas.

Naseem married to Mohammed Mumtaz Abbas and they have four children, Aisha, married to M. Tareq, Asma married to Dr. Yousuf Siddiqui, Shoeb married to Sandy and Asra married to Adil Siddiqui. Aisha has three children, Hana married to M. Faiz; they have two boys Sameer and Ayan. Mona married to W. Syed; they have two boys Deen and Aden. Maryam married to S. Meer, they have one girl Shaila. Asma has two girls and two boys, Adam, Ismael, Reema and Salma. Shoeb has one daughter Shaila. Asra has one boy Zain and one girl Zara.

Nafees married to Viqaruddin Ahmed and they have three children, Shaista, Nisar and Younus. Shaista is marred to M. Moid, Nisar is a Pharmacist in charge at CVS. He is married to Husna, and Younus is married to Samrrea. Shaista has two children Faraz and Samah. Nisar has two children Sumaiya and Mariya. Younus has two children Maaz and Ayaz.

Ather Abbas is a Civil Engineer, married to Naheed and they have two children, Ahmed Abbas and Farheen. Ahmed Abbas is married to Aisha; they have three children, Yousuf, Umer, and Zainab. Farheen is married to M. Kazi, and they have two children, Sahar and Suha.

Najma is married to Mohammed Hakimuddin (Zakir) Siddiqui. They have three children, Minhaj, Husna and Najeeb. Minhaj is married to Barbara, and they have three children, Safia, Jennah, and Sara. Husna is married to Nisar, and they have two children, Sumaiya and Mariya. Najeeb is married to Zinna and they have one child Emal.

Dr. Azher Abbas, a Radiologist, is married to Dr. Shahida, and they have two sons, Adil and Amer, and one daughter, Farah.

6 - Zubaida Begum had no children.

Group Photo of Aziz Jung's Daughters and son-in-laws:

Aziz Jung's Daughters in a family portrait.
Mrs. Deen Yar Jung, center, is also in the photo.

Aziz Jung's son-in-laws in a family portrait.
Deen Yar Jung, center, is also in the photo.

The second daughter of Aziz Jung

Saeedunissa Begum was married to Mohammed Habeebullah the eldest among the three brothers Mohammed Asadullah and Mohammed Valiullah. Their father **Mohammed Ahmedullah** was the brother of **Ahmed Abdul Aziz (Aziz Jung).**

As mentioned earlier, Mohammed Habeebullah is son of Mohammed Ahmedullah, brother of Ahmed Abdul Aziz (Aziz Jung).

Habeebullah was the oldest of the three brothers. Asadullah was his younger brother and Valiullah was the youngest. He was a very sophisticated and handsome man with great personality. He worked as Nazim in Rawramba's Jagir in Osmanabad district. A **Nazim** in Urdu: مظان, means, "Director". Later he worked in 'Small Cause Court' in Hyderabad. Saeedunissa Begum and her husband Mohammed Habeebullah were adored due to their humbleness and love they showed to their relatives. Saeedunissa Begum used to go out of her way to help people and show her love and care towards them. Due to her kindness and pure character she earned the love and respect from all the relatives and friends. She passed away in 1963.

Left to Right: Akberinissa begum, Mohammed Ahmedullah, and their daughter Durdana.

The couple's only child was **Mohammed Ahmedullah**, named after his grandfather. Being the eldest among the cousins everyone referred to him as Bhaijaan. In his house he had a hidden basement also known as ***Teykhana in Urdu,*** which during summer time used to be decorated and all of Ahmedullah's cousins would be anxiously waiting for the moment to lay down there and enjoy the cool and coziness in the hot temperature and getting together with cousins and relatives having a *chitchat,* making the atmosphere an enjoyable and unforgettable one. Saeedunissa Begum used to love he son Ahmedullah very much and thus adored her grandchildren immensely. She had a special bond with her first grandchild Durdana. Even though Naimath and to some extent Shoukath also grew under her care and love, Durdana was appreciated the most. She used to send freshly cooked food in a big Tiffin box for her grandchildren, to St. Georges Grammar School at Abid road, all the way from Aziz Bagh with a servant on bicycle. The food would be served by (Ayah) one of the loyal maids of the family. Other kids would be amazed to see the luxury of hot food being served during lunchtime.

Mohammed Ahmedullah was married to **Akberunnisa Begum**, daughter of Hakeem Mohammed Moizuddin Farooqui, a well known Hakeem, very famous for his Unani medicine 'Zinda Tilismath, and Farooqui Tooth Powder', renown throughout India and especially in Hyderabad. Ahmedullah had eight children, Durdana, Naimath, Rahmath, Farzana, Shoukath, Ruksana, Imrana, and Sadath. He was a very handsome and adorable person. After his Education he worked in different organisations before starting his own business of ready-made garments called **'O.K. Dresses'**. He established his business single-handedly for many years growing from one shop to three shops. Unfortunately due to unforeseen circumstances the business closed down. Later he worked as a Liaison Officer in Coco Cola Company for a number of years. His wife **Akberunnisa Begum** was also called **Dulhan Shehzadi** among elders, because of her prettiness and charm, and as ***Bhabijaan*** among cousins and relatives. She was, and still is, a very pious and lovable lady popular amongst all the relatives. Akberunnisa Begum was the first person who commercially started selling the famous sweet called **"Jaliyaan"**, prepared with Almonds and sugar. Akberunnisa Begum is mashaAllah in good health and gracefully resides in Aziz Bagh. She is regularly visited by the family, children and great grand children, especially getting together during weekends.

Durdana married **Sultan Mahmood**. She has two children, Ahmed Saeed and Humaira (Zubina). Humaira is married to Mohammed.Aliuddin Hyder and have four children, Ayesha, Omer, Sumayya and Fatima. Sayeed is married to Sara and have three children; Zaid, Zaina, and Zoha.

Mr. and Mrs. Ahmedullah with their grandson Ahmed saeed.

Mohammed Naimathullah is married to **Samina Yasmin**, Niece of Sultan Mahmood, daughter of Mahboob Ali, they have three children; Rishad, Mazna, and Atif. Rishad is married to Uzma, they have one daughter Izna. Atif is married to Nimra, daughter of Mir Nizamuddin Ahmed.

Mohammed Rahmathullah is married to **Nuzhath Rahman**, his first cousin, and daughter of Dr. Mahmood-ur-Rehman and Shakeela, sister of Akberunnisa Begum. They have five children; Hafsa, Salwa, Waleed, Sohaib, and Osama, they all reside in U.K. Hafsa is married to Nabeel Khan, and Alim known as Abu Abdis-Salam. They have three children; Zainab, Abdus Salam, and Ali. Salwa is married to Faisal Siddiqui a lecturer in Jeddah. They have three children; Maryam, Abdullah, and Fatima, they live in Makkah Al-Mukarramah.

Farzana is married to **Shamsuddin Ahmed** her second cousin, son of Dr. Hasanuddin Ahmed and Husnara. Farzana has developed the famous sweet 'Badam Ki Jaliyan' into an art by moulding them into the shapes of fruits, greetings and monuments with precision. She has the immense talent of presenting the sweet to match any occasion in Hyderabad. Farzana and Shamsuddin have four children; Fatima, Sameha, Fariya and Naila. Fatima is married to Aqeel. Sameha is married to Hasnain, they have four children; Arman, Ayman, Adnan and Hanan. Fariya is married to Hamed, they have three children; Rayan, Zoya and Zaid.

Mohammed Shoukathullah is married to **Tehmina Anjum**, sister of Samina and daughter of Mahboob Ali. They have three children; Numair, Sanya, and Sama. Sanya is married to Kamran, son of Mir Nizamuddin Ahmed.

Ruksana is married to **Mohammed Fazalullah**, Mohammed Ahmedullah's paternal and maternal cousin from sides, mothers and fathers, and son of Mohammed Valiullah. They have four sons; Habeeb, Mehboob, Safi, and Omer. Habeeb is married to Zakia. Mehboob is married to Safura.

Imrana is married to **Mohammed Mashiatullah**, grandson of Nawab Rahmat Yar Jung. They have three daughters; Sharmeen, Maliha, and Eman. They live in the U.S.A.

Mohammed Sadathullah is married to **Farah Hasan**, daughter of Syed Kurshid-ul-Hasan. They have one daughter, Manal.

Mohammed Ahmedullah's Family.

The third daughter of Aziz Jung

Mumtazunissa Begum married Mohammed Asadullah. He was also Aziz Jung's nephew. He was the District Magistrate in Parbhani and Armoor in Adilabad district. Then he worked for the Asman Jah Paigah also in a District Administration position. He was then the Nazim Umoor Madhabi (Director, Department of Religious Endowments) and twice led delegations of Hujjaj to Makkah on behalf of the Nizam and as a guest of the King of Saudi Arabia.

On one of those occasions Mohammed Asadullah was given the honor of participating in the annual washing of Al Ka'aba and was given a piece of the Kiswatul Ka'aba (Black robe of the Ka'aba) as a souvenir. After his retirement he was a Director of the Nizam's Private Estate.

Mumtazunissa Begum was a devoted wife and an absolute wonder with a personality which included gentleness, steadfastness, exceptional levels of tolerance and endurance. She led a disciplined lifestyle. Her devotion and boundless respect for her husband was exemplary.

As mentioned earlier, Mohammed Asadullah is son of Mohammed Ahmedullah, brother of Ahmed Abdul Aziz (Aziz Jung).

Mohammed Asadullah and his brother-in-law Deen Yar Jung.

Mumtazunissa Begum and Mohammed Asadullah have three daughters, **Akhter** married to Dr. Qadeer, **Iqbal** married to Mirza Abdullah Baig, **Shakira** married to Dr. Anwer Baig.

Dr. Qadeer was the eldest son-in-law of Mohammed Asadullah and Mumtazunissa Begum. He was an Ophthalmologist, and a famous Surgeon. He migrated to Pakistan in the late 1940s. Dr. Qadeer was married to Akhter Jehan, eldest daughter of Mohammed Asadullah

Major Dr. Syed Abdul Qadeer was born on 18th Maarch1914 in Hyderabad Deccan. After completing his M.B.B.S from Osmania University he went for training to U.K where he got his D.O.M.S., F. I. C.S., M. R. C. P., (London) in 1947. He was commissioned in the Pakistan Army as Classified Ophthalmologist, in the rank of Captain. He took premature release from army in 1958, after having operated the then President of Pakistan Sikandar Mirza. Some of his works include his work include his work on Trachoma was published in British Journal of Ophthalmology, published his paper on the treatment of Glaucoma (pressure in eye). He invented a plastic plate, known after his own name. 'Qadeer's Plate', and published the work in British Journal of Ophthalmology, soon the paper was in demand from all quarters of the world. After release from the army he started an Eye Hospital at Rawalpindi.

He introduced the operation of Squint (Crossed eyes) in Pakistan and successfully operated on thousands of patients, and was conferred the Honorary Fellowship of the International College of Surgeons in 1954. Then he moved to Karachi in 1970 where he started his Eye Clinic and worked until the last days of his life. He passed away on 22 January 1992.

Left Mohammed Asadullah and Mumtazunissa Begum with Fazal Qadeer (Mohsin).
Right: Mohammed Asadullah with Ahson, Nafees and Mohsin, 1946.

They have four children, the eldest, Dr. **Nafeesa** Ahmed , married to Moinuddin Ahmed settled in Canada since 1969. Who again have four children, eldest **Nadir** married to Saeeda. Second **Shireen Fatimah**, married to Faraz Rabbani who is an Alim-e-Deen, conducts 'on line' Classes in the Study of Quran called 'Seekers Guidance'. They are blessed with three children Omar Farid and Yasmin. Then Dr. Nafeesa's youngest twins, **Nasiruddin Ahmed** and **Khadiruddin Ahmed.** Nasir is married to Nishat blessed with Daniyal and Khadir is married to Noreen.

Syed Ahsan Quadeer was commissioned in Pakistan Army in 1969 and retired as Lieutenant Colonel in July 1995. **Zarina and Ahsan Quadeer** have three children, the eldest, Shaista Shahkar Sayied married to Shahkar Sayied, they have three children, the eldest is Ammar, the second one Maham, and the youngest is Hannah. Their second daughter, Dr. Tabassum Ahsan Quadeer, an orthodontist is married to Dr. Arshad Hasan who is an Endodontist, they have a son Ahmad. Their youngest daughter, Ayesha Ahsan Quadeer is married to Fahad Aijaz. They live in Achen Germanay where Fahad is doing his Phd. from Achen University in IT.

Fazal Qadeer (Mohsin) Syed Fazal Quadeer (Mohsin) graduated from Gordan College Rawalpindi and then migrated to Canada in 1970. He worked and retired as Technologist in Ontario Power Generation. Mohsin is married to Sadiqa daughter of Ghulam M. Abul Hasan. She did her Masters in History from USA, worked for 29 years for an Insurance company in Canada and retired as Director.

RAISA HASAN is the youngest daughter of Dr. S.A Quadeer and Akhtar Quadeer holds a Bachelor degree in Psychology, married to Dr. Ahmed Hasan E.N.T

Consultant Surgeon with Fellowship from Edinburgh in 1970. He is Currently head of ENT Department Jinnah University of Medical Sciences Karachi.

Four daughters of Raisa Hasan are:
Fariya Sharif herself a graduate of Montessori Education from UK. Currently teaching in Bay View School Karachi. , has one son named Faraz 13 years and daughter Hira 10 years. Fariya is married to Dr. Salman Sharif working as Associate Professor and Surgeon in Liaquat National Hospital. An eminent NEURO SURGEON practicing in Karachi with two fellowships in Neuro surgery from UK published several papers on neuro surgery and spine.

Samiya Sharif is the second daughter she has recently completed Montessori Education course from UK. Has one daughter named Naureen 13 years and son Jibran 8 years. Samiya is married to Irfan Sharif who holds a Bachelors degree in Business Administration from Houston USA and currently involved in his own Fashion House and Garment business in Karachi

Sana Badshah is the third daughter; she is a medical doctor with graduation from DMC Karachi. Has one son named Usman 4 years. She is married to Dr. Faisal Badshah who is a professional Psychiatrist working in UK.

Muna Ahmed is the youngest she has completed her Bachelors in Information Technology and a second major in Business and Tourism from Emirates Academy of Hospitality Management – Dubai. this is affiliated to LOUSANNE Institute Switzerland. Currently she is working as Business Development Manager in London with BMI - UK. She is married to Ahmed Bozai who is a professional Banker working as Vice President Citi Group – UK. He holds two post graduation in Business Administration one from IBA – Karachi and the other from London - UK

Mirza Abdullah Baig was married to Iqbal Unissa Begum, and they had four children. He was one of the most pious/honest and humble member of family and he was known for his simplicity and humility. Abdullah Baig was in civil service and worked in Bangalore, he retired as Deputy Commissioner.

He was very interested in History and particularly Islamic History. The untimely loss of his son Arifullah Baig during his life was the ultimate testing and painful life event for him and remains a gap in the hearts and lives of his sisters till this day and a regular sad and painful reminder for Iqbal Unnissa Begum. Iqubal Unnissa Begum is at present the most senior member of Aziz Bagh family. She is blessed with a uniquely positive and forward thinking personality and a zest for gaining new and modern skills, one of the few from her generation to use internet to communicate, while teaching and imparting to the youngsters the true wealth of cultural and old traditional values. Arifullah has left behind two children, Noorain and Hussnain who are both doing well under the guidance of their mother Munawar Baig. Abdullah Baig passed away in May 2007.

Habeeba married to Majeed Khan and they have three children. Ausia, married to Dr. Fayaz Malik who is a Cardiologist at Heartcare Midwest, Peoria, IL. They have three children Kasim, Imaan, Hasan.

Lateef Khan (Haris), Program manager and Business Analyst at GE Healthcae at Milwaukee, WI. He is married to Ayesha who is HumanResource Manager of Diagnostic Ultra Sound IT at GE and they have two children, Sa'ad and Amani. Mubeen is Strategic Planning Manager for Caterpillar Financial Services Division at Nashville, TN and he has one girl, Mariam.

Four generations: Left to Right Iqbal, Habiba, Ausia and Imaan.

From Left to Right: Azra, Asad, Hena and Waheed.

Dr. Azra Tanweer married to Dr. Waheed Sabir. They moved to UK in 1974 and they are both based in Cardiff, Wales. Dr. Azra is a Consultant in NHS UK and Dr. Waheed Sabir is a Medical practitioner. Their son Dr. Asad Zubair Sabir is married to Dr. Hena and they are based in Birmingham and proud parents of Idris Taha Sabir who is 6 months old.

Dr. Mirza Anwer Baig, married the youngest daughter of Mohammad Asadullah, Shakira in 1954. Dr. Anwer Baig qualified in Medicine from Madras Medical College, Madras and worked for the Government of Mysore for a number of years. He then decided to settle in Hyderabad which was also his hometown and joined Hyderabad Allwyn Metal Works as Medical Officer. He worked there for more over 15 years. On retirement he worked for a few years with Princess Asra Hospital as Resident Medical Officer and Administrator for the hospital. He was a surgeon and physician.

Shakira Anwer, his wife taught her children to read the Qur'an and gave them the tools to succeed in life. All her children and grandchildren are doing well in India and the US. She now has a little great-grandson, Mohammad Anas Rumman.

They have five children;
Mirza Yawar Baig is President, Yawar Baig and Associates, in India. He is married to Samina Baig.
Atiya Fatima Mohiuddin married to Maqdoom Mohiuddin, Professor, Osmania University. He passed away in 2006. They have three children, Safia Fatima, Shaheen Fatima, Sara Fatima.
Mirza Muzaffer Baig is Advisor in Wealth Management and Investment, in USA. He is married to Patricia Baig, and they have twins, Marya Baig and Sarah Baig.
Shamsa Fatima is a Hospital Administrator in USA and is married to Sajid Khan.
Zakia Fatima is a teacher in Hyderabad, India.

The fourth daughter of Aziz Jung

Fasiullah Hussaini and Aijazunnisa

Aijazunissa in 2002

Aijazunissa Begum married to Moulana Syed Shah Fasiullah Hussaini Baghdadi Quadri, Sajjada Nasheen Dargah-e-Chincholi who at the time of marriage had two children Syed Hashim Hussaini (Saheballah) and Syeda Khairunnisa (Muneer) with his late wife. They together had six children, three daughters and three sons.

The entire Hussaini family lived together at Hashim Manzil, a block away from Aziz Bagh until 1960. Later on, they built and moved into a house in Aziz Bagh.

Fasiullah Hussaini (born 12 April 1904) also known as Murshad Jaani was the son of Hazrath Syed Mohammed Baghdadi (Manjle Baghdadi). Manjle Baghdadi along with his brother Hazrath Syed Abdur Rahman Baghdadi (Bade Baghdadi) migrated from Baghdad during the era of Mir Mahboob Ali Khan (Nizam VI). The Nizam who respected scholars used to respect and honor both Bade Baghdadi and Manjle Baghdadi Saheb, and granted them an honorarium. Fasiullah Hussaini got education at Jamia Nizamia where he completed Maulvi Alim & Maulvi Kamil. He worked as an Islamic studies teacher at Ghosha Mahal high school and later he worked with Dairatul Muareef. He had Khilafat from Bade Baghdadi Saheb in the Sufi Tareqa of Quadria and from his maternal Grand father in the Tariqa of Chistia. From his childhood he had a great attachment to the Holy Quran. It is said that he used to go to the Masjid for I'tekaf and would return after reading the whole Quran. He made a lifelong habit of getting up at 4:00 am and reciting almost 10 Juz every day. Being a Khalifa of the great Shaykhs he inherited compassion and love for people, especially for the residents of Taluka Chincholi and its vicinity. Once a year at the anniversary (Urs) of his maternal grandfather, he would send an open invitation for a meal (lunger) from early morning to noon. Thousands of people would attend. He also used to invite non-Muslims of Chincholi for a Tea Party a day before. The result of all this hospitality was that the whole community used to feel very close to him, and he used to consider them as his own children. One of the residents of Chincholi, Veerender Patel became the Chief Minister of Karnataka. Veerender Patel always had a very affectionate relationship and a high regard for Moulana Fasiullah Hussaini. Needy and helpless people used to visit Moulana at home looking for help. He would spend money out of his own pocket, and take them to Gulbarga and Bangalore to get them jobs or to resolve their issues. He spent most of his days reciting Quran and doing Kidmate Khalq (service to mankind), especially for the people residing in the rural areas of Chincholi and in Hyderabad. He passed away on 27th December, 1983. His funeral was attended by thousands of people in Chincholi, where he was buried.

Aijazunissa Begum lovingly known as Munnu was born on 9th April 1909. She MashaAllah lived a long and fulfilling life, and was lucky to witness four generations in her lineage. She was a woman of character and strength. Not only did she care for her loved ones, but also made it a point to help them, always keeping in mind their best interest. She would perform any tasks entrusted upon her, whether it was arrangements for a marriage, organizing family events, or taking total responsibility for the annual visit to Chincholi for the anniversary (Urs). To travel 100 miles in those days would require four means of transportation--starting with a tricycle (rickshaw) from home to Nampally, a train from Hyderabad to Tandur, a bus from Tandur to Chincholi, and a cart from the bus station to the house. Just the journey to Chincholi used to take 10 hours. Arranging the logistics for the family of almost 25 people, with luggage and food during travel, to reside in Chincholi for 15 days, while hosting almost 150 people, was a humongous task to be accomplished. All the arrangements for boarding and lodging (including the beds that had to be carried) were made from Hyderabad. It was always her foremost priority to help host family members and many others. Not only was she a woman with a big heart, she was also a woman of wisdom and intellect. In a time when a girl's education was given little preference, she was raised with an honorable education at home, which included speaking and writing fluent Urdu and also some English, Arabic and Persian. Being the eldest among her in-laws, she was extremely well known and respected by them. Due to her attachment to the family, she had all four of her sons marry within the family. One of the most memorable qualities about her was her hospitality. Her face would light up at the sight of visitors, especially her nieces and nephews, and her duas and blessings would soon follow. She passed away peacefully on 19th December 2004 and was buried in Chincholi.

Syed Hashim Hussaini Baghdadi (Saheballah) married to Syeda Shareefa Baafaqeeh (Moin Sahebzadi), niece of Fasiullah Hussaini. They had five children – Ayesha, Akbar, Shaheen, Nasreen and Mujeeb. Hashim Hussaini passed away in 1986. Moin Sahebzadi is residing in Houston ,USA with Ayesha, Akbar and Mujeeb.

Syeda Khairunnisa (Muneer) is married to Syed Azizullah Hussaini. They have four sons Khaleel, Junaid, Zubair and Shibli. All of them are residing in Chicago, USA.

Syeda Kaneez Fatima (Madani) married to Dr. Mohammed Abdul Quddus Siddiqui son of Hakeem Mohammed Azam who was a retired professor in Unani medicine and was also a personal physician to the Nizam. Dr. Quddus did his M.B.B.S from Osmania University and holds a postgraduate diploma in tuberculosis and chest disease. He served in various capacities at the government TB hospital in Hyderabad. He has also been running his private clinic at his residence Quddus Manzil two blocks away from Aziz Bagh for the past six decades. Madani has a very kind hearted, lovable and angelic personality. They had two daughters Shahnaz, and Shahida, and one son Dr. Mohammed Abdul Qadeer Siddiqui. Shahnaz is married to Syed Imaduddin Tariq and they have a daughter and a son Mariam Tariq and Ali Tariq. Ali is married to Shabana. Dr. Qadeer Siddiqui is married to Dr. Jabeen and they have three children, Buthul Siddqui, Azam Siddqui and Amthul Siddqui.

Muneer, Madani, Asghar,Tahira, Hajira   Quddus & Madani   Quddus & Azam

Syed Mohammed Hussaini Baghdadi (Pasha) married to Syeda Hameedunissa (Nafees), daughter of Moulana Syed Abdul Rahim Hussaini Baghdadi and niece of Fasiullah Hussaini. They have one son, Syed Ali Abbas Hussaini (Mansoor). Mohammed Hussaini did his graduation in Agriculture from Osmania University and MSc in Agriculture from Andhra Pradesh Agriculture University. He served as an Assistant and Associate Professor. He also taught graduate and postgraduate students at Agriculture College. He was a renowned and popular science teacher among his undergraduate students who are now doctors, engineers and civil servants. Besides his academic attainments he was a good sportsman, and a sports champion of his college in athletics. He was the captain of the O.U. Cricket team and represented his university in Inter-university championship held at Baroda in 1956. He is one of the very few people in the family who managed to attend the Aziz Jung Mosque everyday regularly for prayers for almost four decades. His son, Mansoor is married to Nasreen and they have three children, Syed Saifuddin Hussaini (Saif), Syed Aliuddin Hussaini (Ali), and Syeda Aijaz Fatima (Maliha).

Pasha & Nafees

Ali, Nafees, Nasreen, Maliha, Mansoor, Saif, Pasha

Syeda Manzoor Fatima (Tahira) married to Syed Shah Mazhar Hussaini Saberi son of Maulana Syed Shah Saber Hussaini. Mazhar Hussaini graduated from Osmania University where he was one of the leading athletes and won weight lifting & wrestling championships. He is a businessman who started his business with optical merchandise in the mid sixties which he later expanded with his five sons into franchises known as "Saberi's Opticals", "Spects World", and "Shades" having more than 25 outlets at various locations in Hyderabad and neighboring cities. Moulana Syed Shah Mazhar Hussaini, Sajjada Nasheen is Mushir-e-alla of All India Jamiyatul Mashaeq. He is the president of Masjid-e-Ghousia (Farhathnagar) where he has been giving Jummah Qutba (Friday Sermon) since the 80's. Tahira Just like her mother is very family oriented and extremely generous. She encourages family gatherings and frequently invites family members especially those coming from abroad at their farm house. Their five sons are – (1)Syed Mahmood Hussaini Saberi (Hussaini) married to Nishath. They have five children - Ali Mohsin, Sana, Farah, Hina, and Ali Imran. (2) Syed Mohammed Hussaini Saberi (Hassan) is married to Yasmin and they have four children - Ali Asghar, Ali Ather, Saba and Ali Hyder. (3) Syed Hamed Hussaini Saberi (Hamed) married to Faria. They have three children- Ali Riyan, Zoya, Zaid. (4) Syed Ahsanullah Hussaini Saberi (Hasnain) is married to Sameha and they have four children – Ali Arman, Aiman, Ali Adnan and Ali Hannan. (5) Ali Akber is the youngest.

Hussaini

Hassan

Hamed

Hasnain

Ali Akber

Syed Ahmed Hussaini Baghdadi married to Pervin Jehan Siddiqui, daughter of Abida (Niece of Aijazunissa) and Professor Naimuddin Siddiqui. They have two daughters. Ayesha, is married to Jawad Anwar. They have four children –Hefsa, Maaria, Rumaysa (who passed away during infancy), and Yasir. Khadija is married to Hafidh Asim Kazi. Ahmed Hussaini is a Mechanical Engineer with a BE from Osmania University and an MS from Old Dominion University (Virginia). He started working for the International Division of GE in 1980, installing and servicing gas turbines in several countries in the Middle East. As a Chief Mechanical Engineer, he was responsible for installing two gas turbines at the Makkah Power Station which supplies 140 MW of electricity to the Haram. In 1986 he joined Chrysler Motors (Detroit, Michigan) as a Robotics Engineer; later on taking up the position of Senior Process Engineer, Advance Manufacturing Engineering. From the very beginning, Ahmed Hussaini has been a very pious and God-fearing person. His humility, simplicity, and devout love for our beloved Prophet Mohammed (PBUH) is worth mentioning. A conversation with him always includes either some words of wisdom, a hadith, the meaning of an ayah from the Quran, or a poetic verse of Allama Iqbal. His uniqueness lies in the fact that like our dear Prophet he believes in doing. He and his whole family have mashallah made Islam as their true way of life and try their best to live by the Quran and Sunnah.

Pervin Hussaini has a diploma from the University of London in English literature. She was in the Shura of a major Muslim organization in America. She has traveled to different states to give lectures on different Islamic topics. Her lectures have played on local radio stations. She has traveled to Syria with both Ayesha and Khadija, and was solely responsible for their schooling in Jamia Abu Noor and Jamia Damascus. Because of her linguistic skills she became very close to the daughter of the Grand Mufti of Syria. Her efforts led to Ayesha getting admission in the undergraduate program of Jamia Abu Noor, and Khadija getting her Ijaza in Tajweed from the famous Qari & Shaik Abu Hassan Khurdi. The certificate (Ijaza) did not mention her name; instead naming her father per tradition (always a reason for complaint with her!)

Syeda Aziz Fatima (Hajira) married to Khaja Fakhruddin (Aziz) son of Khaja Muneeruddin, Reader, Head of Department of History (Osmania University). Khaja Fakhruddin studied BSC (Hons) in Chemical Engineering at University of London. He specialized in Oil/ Gas processing onshore/offshore and field development and traveled extensively world over working in the capacity of consulting Principle/Lead Process Engineer with Internationally known UK contractors. He read papers in International symposiums organized by Professional Institutes and Universities and his hobbies are reading and writing. Hajira established a boutique in London in the mid 80's and is currently running it under the name of "Hina Boutique." She has Mashallah been able to build her successful business over the years with immense hard work and perseverance. Her welcoming nature gave many of the family members a chance to visit London especially for those traveling from India to America or vice versa. They have two sons Zia & Shuja and a daughter Hina Fatima.

Aziz

Shuja , Zia & Hajira

Syed Asghar Hussaini Baghdadi (Munna) married to Syeda Zehra Hussaini daughter of Moulana Syed Noorullah Hussaini and Syeda Tajunnissa (niece of Fasiullah Hussaini). Asghar Hussaini did his graduation (B.Com) from Osmania University. He lived in Jeddah, Saudi Arabia from 1977 to 2002, and worked in the airport services for Attar Travel at Jeddah International Airport. Through his job he had the opportunity to meet and serve a number of our relatives, friends, celebrities, politicians, and scholars visiting the Kingdom for Hajj and Umrah. He is known for his unique talents and hobbies. Since a very young age he started collecting a variety of things such as stamps, coins, currency notes, stationery, magazines and miniature cars just to name a few. He later developed a keen interest in scrap booking and now has a collection of hand made books with news articles covering key events from the past few decades to the present. For developing such notable reference books, he was awarded the "Best Reader Award" by the Indian Readers Forum in 1998 in Jeddah. Due to his love for travel, he went on around the world trip twice, once by himself in 1980 and later in 1985 with Zehra and Zainab. One of the most heartwarming deeds he was able to accomplish was the reunion of his mother Aijazunnissa with her youngest sister Khursheedunnisa after almost 30 years, when he took her to Karachi in 1983. He was able to fulfill his mother's wish when he performed Hajj-e-Badal for her father Aziz Jung in 1981, and later for her mother Aziz Fatima (Mohammedi Daadi Maa) in 1983 respectively. He is currently residing with his family in Los Angeles, California. They have three children, Syeda Zainab Hussaini, Syed Omar Hussaini and Syeda Sakina Hussaini. Zainab is married to Hafidh Syed Abdul Azeem

(Adnan), Pharm.D and they have two children, Haneefah Fatima Syed and Huzaifa Ahmed Syed.

Asghar ,Zainab ,Zehra, Omar, Sakina

Standing: Omar, Sakina. Sitting: Adnan, Asghar, Huzaifa, Zehra, Haneefah Zainab

The fifth daughter of Aziz Jung

Vahidunissa Begum, married to Mohammed Valiullah, former Sessions Judge and District Magistrate. He was also Aziz Jung's nephew.

As mentioned earlier, Mohammed Valiullah is son of Mohammed Ahmedullah, brother of Ahmed Abdul Aziz (Aziz Jung).

Sitting Left to Right: Muhammad Khalilullah, Akhtar Khalil, Rabia, Mohammed Valiullah, Vahidunissa Begum, Zahida Aziz and Aziz Ahmed. Standing Left to Right: Abida Siddiqui, Muhammad Anwarullah, Mohammed Fazalullah, Mahmooda Ahson. Sitting on the carpet: Jaweed Aziz, Mohammed Zafarullah and Amina Ahmed.

Mohammed Valiullah was born in 1898 in Hyderabad, and was the youngest of the three brothers in the family. He lost his father Mohammed Ahmedullah at an early age and was raised by his paternal uncle Nawab Aziz Jung Bahadur.

Valiullah graduated in 1922 with a bachelor's degree in Law (BA/ LLB) from Osmania University, Hyderabad. During 1925, he was married to Vahidunissa Begum daughter of Nawab Aziz Jung Bahadur and they were blessed with seven children and twenty-three grandchildren.

Valiullah progressed through his professional law career working for the Government of Hyderabad in several districts, before finally working until retirement as the District Magistrate and Session Judge in the Hyderabad courts. Upon his retirement from the government service, he was appointed as the legal adviser to the private estate of the Nizam of Hyderabad and worked there until 1965.

He enjoyed playing sports that included tennis, bridge and chess. During his retirement years he played chess extensively with his cousin brother Ruknuddin Ahmed and his other family members.
He passed away at age 81 on Sept 19, 1979 at his home in Aziz Bagh, Hyderabad, India.

Vahidunissa Begum, daughter of Nawab Aziz Jung Bahadur and Amtullah Begum was born in 1909 and got married to her cousin Mohammed Valiullah in 1925.

Though Vahidunissa Begum did not go through the formal education process, she had the opportunity to grow with her close family in Aziz Bagh, and as a consequence gained invaluable insights into developing into an extremely helpful and dedicated individual.

She was very close to her children and grandchildren as well. Some of her grandchildren would come to stay with her during their summer vacations. To this day, the grand-children talk about how she would take care of their every need and would give them money to go to movies, buy kites, rent bicycles, etc. She also had a very mild manner and would never get upset or scold her children or grand-children. She always taught her children and grand children to develop and maintain special relationships with all family members, and set that example by displaying these qualities herself.

Some of the qualities that she had included helping others first, cooking delicious meals and sending food to her extended family members, helping the poor, giving away gifts that she would receive to her children and other family members, and never complaining.
She had an extremely congenial personality and was loved by her immediate and extended family members.

On September 2, 1984, she quietly passed away in her sleep.

Mohammed Valiullah and Vahidunissa Begum have four sons and three daughters, namely:

Rasheedunissa Begum (Zahida) was the eldest daughter married to Aziz Ahmed the third son of Ahmed Hussain Juddy. Aziz Ahmed graduated from Osmania University and then proceeded on a scholarship for higher education to Manchester, UK and obtained a Degree in Civil Engineering with Honours.

On his return to India, he was appointed as an Assistant Engineer in the Municipal Corporation of Hyderabad. Through his hard work, dedication and expertise in the area of RCC Design of multi-storied buildings and development of roads, he was deputed as city engineer responsible for development of roads and buildings for the entire city of Hyderabad. Within a short period of few years, he progressed to the position of Superintending Engineer for the Housing Board. His honesty and integrity was of a very high order, and was recognized in every office he worked, and the individuals that he dealt with. Even today, when people come to know Jaweed Aziz as his son who is following in his father's professional line of work, they stand in reverence and praise him for his integrity and technical expertise. The roads, multi-storey buildings which he designed and executed in Hyderabad are a true testimony to his honesty, integrity and technical expertise. He was the Superintending Engineer at the time of his sudden and shocking demise in October 1963.

Late Rasheedunissa Begum and Aziz Ahmed have two sons, and one daughter, Jaweed Aziz, Amina Ahmed and Shahid Aziz. **Jaweed Aziz** the eldest son is married to Ruqaiya daughter of Late Azizuddin Ahmed. He completed his Civil Engineering degree in first division with distinction in 1976. For a number of years,

Jaweed has been doing consultancy work in structural engineering. With his hard work and integrity like his father, he has been very successful in his professional career and has designed and executed a number of high rise buildings and shopping complexes in Hyderabad. Jaweed and Ruqaiya has one son (Arshad) and two daughters (Ayesha and Salma). Arshad, B.E, MS in Structural Engineering is married to Nishat, and they have one daughter Muneeba. Ayesha is married to Imad Ahmed (son of Amina and Dr. Mohammed Ahmed).

Amina Ahmed is married to **Mohammed Ahmed**, MD, one of the 11 children of Ahmed Abdul Khadir and Aziz Fatima. (**Note**: Ahmed Abdul Khadir is the son of Ismatunissa Begum, elder sister of Amtullah Begum- Deen Yar Jung's mother). Mohammed Ahmed is a Fellow of American College of Physicians (FACP), Fellow of American College of Endocrinologists (FACE), Fellow of Royal College of Physicians. He is an author of 58 full length research papers in international peer-reviewed journals, presented 122 abstracts in international meetings and delivered over 200 invited lectures. He is a consultant Endocrinologist at the King Faisal Specialist Hospital & Research Center in Riyadh , Saudi Arabia.

Amina & Mohammed Ahmed have three children: Imad Ahmed, Ali Imran Ahmed, & Sara Fatima. **Imad**, JD/MPA/DPA (Vice-President of United Health, Minneapolis) is married to Ayesha (daughter of Jaweed Aziz) and they have three children: Sumayya, Hufsa and Sana. **Ali Imran**, Patent Attorney-At-Law based in Chicago is married to Sameera (daughter of Mohammed Zafarullah), and they have one son: Momin.

Shahid Aziz migrated in 1977 from Hyderabad, India to Minnesota, USA. With his hard work and dedication over a number of years, he has been a very successful businessman and entrepreneur in Minnesota. He is married to Nilofer, and they have three children: Mariam, Ahmed and Omar.

Professor Muhammad Khalilullah is the eldest son of Vahidunissa Begum who completed his post graduation in Political Science from Osmania University, Hyderabad, India. He then migrated to Karachi, Pakistan in the early 1950's and started his career in education with Urdu College, and over the years progressed from a lecturer to Professor and retired as Principal of the same college. During the course of his professional career, he wrote several books on Political Science, International Relations, Tajweed etc.

He has to his credit more than fifteen books, several of them are prescribed in the Bachelors and Master Curriculum of Karachi University. He Served as Dean Faculty of Law, University of Karachi and during his tenure as Dean, was responsible for starting Masters teaching in Law (LLM). He was nominated and served as Member of Syndicate University of Karachi. He has the distinction of meeting and presenting his books to Pakistan President Ayub Khan and President General Zia Ul Haq. He participated in Hyderabad 'Serat' Conference as a representative of President Zia Ul Haq.

Professor Khalilullah has followed in his grandfather's literary footsteps by becoming the author of several books written in urdu. As research director, he is also honoured to have supervised 10 of the 17 theses selected for the Supreme Court of Pakistan library by the Chief Justice of Pakistan. And many of his students have gone on to achieve positions of great stature in the country.

In 1993 he was awarded two fellowships an FIBA and FABI. He was also conferred with award of gold medal NISHAN URDU by the Ministry of Education, Government of Pakistan. His articles were a regular feature in all the main newspapers of Karachi, and is a very literary and distinguished personality among the educational elite of the City. He Served as the Honorary President of Osmania Old Boys Association Karachi, and was on the Board of Trustees of various Educational Organizations. Currently due to his poor health, he refrains from social and educational activities. Muhammad Khalilullah is married to **Akhtar Khalil**, eldest daughter of Dr. Muhammad Haseen (Civil Surgeon in Hyderabad), and they have three children: Humayun Khalil, Rabiya and Zehra. They had another son Irfan who passed away in his infancy.

Humayun Khalil, the eldest son is a Professional Consulting Architect and Associate Partner with Parc International. He completed his post graduation in Architecture from Grad School of Architecture, University of Utah, Salt Lake City in 1982. During his studies in USA, he excelled and was awarded the American Institute of Architect Student Gold Medal for best student 1982, and the Deans Award of Best Design Research Thesis. He had completed his B.Arch from N.E.D university Karachi in 1979 securing First Class First position and was awarded the Gold Medal. Over the years, Humayun has demonstrated his professionalism and technical expertise in designing and executing complex Architecural projects in U.A.E., Pakistan, Khartoum, Oman, Morocco and Lebanon.

Rabia Shujaat is married to **Shujaat Siddique** a professional Acturist with education in Acturial Science from UK. They have two sons, Shoaib and Omair. The elder son, Shoaib, MBA is married to Sadia, MBA, and they one son Shaheryar.

Zehra Ahson, M.D. a doctor by profession is married to Haseeb Ahson the eldest son of Mahmoodunissa Begum. Zehra had completed her initial requirements of Medicine in the States and has opted for research oriented work in Medicine. Haseeb is a professional Civil Engineer from N.E.D University Karachi with a Masters in Transportation Engineering from University of Utah, Salt Lake City. Over the past several years, Haseeb has been very successful in his professional career and has been running an Engineering and Transportation Studies consulting firm, TechniQuest Corporation with offices in New Jersey and New York. Zehra and Haseeb has a daughter Anum and son Zohair.

Dr. Muhammad Anwarullah completed his Master's degree in Zoology with first division from Osmania University Hyderabad, India. After migrating to Pakistan in 1956, he joined Pakistan Council of Scientific and Industrial Research (PCSIR Karachi Labs) as a Technical Assistant. In 1960, he went to Germany on a Scholarship from the Ministry of Education and received his PhD. in (Acorology) Entomology from Hohenheim Agriculture Univ. in Stuttgart, West Germany. He continued as Chief Scientific Officer (CSO) & Head of the Department of Applied Biology and Marine Research Division of PCSIR Karachi, Pakistan.

He retired in 1992. Muhammad Anwarullah, like all his other siblings, had a very special inclination towards education and religion. He was very much known amongst his peers as a studious and a quite person. While others were playing in Aziz Bagh grounds, he would be seen sitting at a side busy enjoying his books. Amongst his extra curricular activities, he was a Chess Champion at the Osmania University, spoke German, visited several countries, attended various National and International Seminars and Meetings and wrote 50 research papers that were published in national and International Journals and many popular scientific articles published in local newspapers and magazines.

He published a booklet on termites proofing of buildings, pesticides and pest control in English and Noor-e-Hidayat, Khandeel, Usool-e-Zindagi and Aqwal-e-Zarrin in Urdu. He received a gold medal from Agriculture Research Council of Pakistan for developing an indigenous pesticide for termites known as **PETKOLIN,** and was also awarded a gold medal from the American Association of Scientist in recognition of his scientific achievements. His name was also published in the top 500 Personalities of the World.
Muhammad Anwarullah is married to **Salma Anwar**, daughter of Dr. Muhammad Haseen, and they have three children, Fatima, Ali and Jawad.

Fatima Athar a doctor by profession, works in the Medical Research Industry in New Jersey. Fatima is married to Muhammad Intikhab Athar, who is a Professional Civil Engineer from NED University in Karachi. He completed his Master's degree in Transportation from the University of Utah, Salt Lake City, and has been working for the past several years for an Engineering Consultancy firm in New Jersey. Fatima and Intikhab have three sons: Ammar, Ebad and Saad.

Ali Anwar, is a doctor cum DBA (Database Administrator), works as a DB Manager for a local semi government company that overlooks Karachi Stock Exchange Online Transactions. Ali is married to Saima and they have three sons: Muhtashim, Rayaan and Hassan.

Jawad Anwar migrated to California, USA in 1997 after completing his Master's degree in Computer Science from the University of Karachi. After working for a number of years for a Software Consulting firm in California, Jawad now works for an Online Marketing Analytics company in Ann Arbor Michigan as a Software Engineer. Jawad is married to Ayesha (daughter of Perveen and Syed Ahmed Hussaini), and they have two daughters and one son namely: Hefsa, Maaria, and Yasir. Their third daughter, Rumaysa sadly passed away in her infancy.

Zaibunissa Begum (Abida) married Mohammed Naimuddin Siddiqui son of Mohammed Burhanuddin Siddiqui in 1956. Professor Naimuddin Siddiqui received his Master of Arts degree in English from Osmania University in Hyderabad, India and was granted a scholarship to study at Oxford University. He completed his MA (Honors) from Oxford University and returned to India where he taught English at Osmania University for 25 years. He migrated to West Africa in 1969 where he taught English Language & Literature as a Professor at the University of Liberia in Monrovia, Liberia for 10 years. Due to political instability in Liberia, he migrated to California in June 1979, where he lived for the rest of his life. After his retirement in California, he devoted his time to reading and writing literary works. His publications besides poetry, include fiction and literary works, and he was the recipient of Awards in English Poetry in the United States. He participated in Urdu Mushairas for the Urdu Markaz International. In response to a long-felt need, he made the first English Verse Translation of *Iqbal's Baal-i-Jibreel* in 1996.

Professor Naimuddin Siddiqui's modesty and humbleness cannot be characterized in words. He had a great selfless desire to help people and he was often sought for his expertise and mastery, not only in English, Urdu, but also other languages such as *Farsi* (Persian). He often emphasized that it was not sufficient for one to read and master only in your field of expertise, but that it is necessary to strike a balance and be well-versed and knowledgeable in multiple disciplines. His devotion to other subjects including Islam is evidenced in his meticulous study of the*Siraat-al-Nabi*(Sahih Al-Bukhari and Sahih Muslim) as he was preparing to compose the *Siraat-al-Nabi* translation. Abida Begum and Mohammed Naimuddin Siddiqui have three children, Pervin, Zaheer and Tasneem.

Perveen Hussaini is married to Syed Ahmed Hussaini, and they have two daughters: Ayesha and Khadija. Syed Ahmed Hussaini is the son of Aziz Jung's daughter, Aijazunissa Begum. Ahmed's details can be found in Aijazunissa Begum's section of the book.

Ayesha is married to Jawad (son of Dr.Muhammad Anwarullah), and they have two daughters and one son namely: Hefsa, Maaria, and Yasir. Their third daughter, Rumaysa sadly passed away in her infancy. **Khadija** is married to Hafiz Asim Kazi.

Mohammed Zaheeruddin Siddiqui graduated with a degree in Electronics Engineering from California and worked in the computer industry for over 12 years before starting his own Software Consulting firm, **Completech** in the San Francisco Bay Area. He is married to Asfia Khan who has a Bachelor's degree in Software Engineering, and worked as Director of Software Quality Assurance before moving into Software Consulting. Zaheer and Asfia have three children: Omar, Nadia and Amer.

Tasneem Jehan Sayeed graduated with a Bachelor's degree in Computer Science from California Polytechnic University in Pomona, California. She moved to the San Francisco Bay area in December 1990. She has made significant contributions at several major software corporations in the capacity as a Mobile Software Architect, Technology Manager, Senior Director and Vice President of Engineering. She currently works for the Symbian Foundation, which is headquartered in London, UK, with offices in Foster City, California, China and Japan. Tasneem Sayeed is married to Mohammed Sadath Sayeed, son of Mohammed Asadullah Sayeed (IAS Officer) and Zahra Shehnaz Sayeed. (**Note**: Asadullah Sayeed's mother Aftab Begum was the sister of Amtullah Begum, wife of Aziz Jung.) Mohammed Sadath Sayeed graduated with a Master of Science degree in Computer Engineering from San Jose State University in California. After working for several large corporations in California in the field of Software Quality Assurance for a number of years, he is now providing consulting engineering services for major corporations. Tasneem and Sadath have two daughters: Yasmin and Maryam.

Mahmoodunissa Begum (Mahmooda) the youngest of the 3 daughters of Vahidunissa Begum married Mohammad Ahson elder son of Dr. Muhammad Haseen.

Mohammad Ahson, an accountant by Profession, did his Bachelors in Commerce from University of Karachi, started his carrier with M/s FORD RHODES of Pakistan. After completing his articleship passed the Chartered Accountancy exam and later became the Fellow of The Institute of Chartered Accountants of Pakistan. (i.e FCA). He joined M/s Rafhan Maize Products affiliated to CPC International New Jersey in the capacity as Financial Officer and as a result migrated to Lyallpur now known as Faisalabad. Through his hard work, dedication and professionalism, he very quickly progressed through his career to become the CFO of Rafhan. He migrated back to Karachi and joined Premier Tobacco Co. as the Chief Financial Manager of Premier Tobacco Co in 1980. Mohammad Ahson was a very widely traveled and well exposed person, a strict disciplinarian and well known for his punctuality and immaculate dressing. Socially, he was a very popular figure in the social elite circles of Faisalabad. He was an active member of Rotary International and held many honorary positions in Rotary and Elite Chenab Club of Faisalabad. He was a keen reader of magazines from his student life and used to have a large collection of 'Readers Digest' and 'National Geographics' from late 1960's onwards till 1982. As an enthusiast of sports, he was always involved in active participation and infact, his sudden and shocking demise was on the tennis court of KMC Sport complex, Karachi on 28th April 1982. Mahmooda Begum and Mohammad Ahson have three children: Haseeb, Habib and Huma.

Haseeb Ahson is a professional Civil Engineer from N.E.D University Karachi with a Master's degree in Transportation Engineering from University of Utah, Salt Lake City. Over the past several years, Haseeb has been very successful in his professional career and has been running an Engineering and Transportation Studies consulting firm, TechniQuest Corporation with offices in New Jersey and New York.

Haseeb is married to Zehra,MD (daughter of Muhammad Khalilullah), and they have a daughter Anum and son Zohair.

Habib Ahson had completed a Bachelor's degree in Commerce from University of Karachi. He migrated to New Jersey in 1994 and completed a Bachelor's degree in Finance from Seton Hall University in New Jersey. After working for several years for a computer consulting firm in California, he moved back to New Jersey and currently works as a Senior Project Manager for TechniQuest Corporation.

Habib is married to Kishwer, and they have two children: Sarah and Abdallah.

Huma Ahmed a doctor by profession works as a licenced surgical assistant in Chicago. She is married to Dr. Ali Ahmed, MD, PhD son of Habib and Nasreen Ahmed, and they have four children: Imaan, Zayd, Adil and Yusuf.

Mohammed Fazalullah graduated with a Bachelor's degree in Science from Osmania University. He went on to obtain a degree in Civil Engineering from Guindy Engineering College in Tamil Nadu (former Madras) in 1964. Upon his graduation, he started to work for Corporation of Madras as an Engineering Supervisor. During his 19 years of service with Corporation he progressed through the ranks of Asssitant Engineer and then promoted to an Executive Engineer, Bridges work department. Upon the death of his father Mohammed Valiullah in September 1979, he moved back to his hometown, Hyderabad to take care of his mother Vahidunissa Begum. He pursued Civil Engineering Consulting work in Hyderabad for few years before proceeding to Saudi Arabia to take on the position of a Resident Civil Engineer. After working for five years in Jeddah, Saudi Arabia, he moved to Al Ain, UAE and worked there for twelve years as a Resident Engineer. After completing almost 17 years of Professional Engineering service in the Middle East, he returned back to Hyderabad. He is currently retired and devotes his time in social work helping out the needy people. He is an excellent chess player and represented Hyderabad State in the National Student Chess Championship held in Madras in 1959. Mohammed Fazalullah is married to Rukhsana (daughter of Mohammed Ahmedullah), and they have four sons: Habib, Mehboob, Safi and Omar.

His eldest son **Habib** upon completing his Bachelor's degree in Computer Engineering from India, migrated to Australia in 2003 and obtained a Master's degree in Information Technology from La Trobe University. He currently is working in Melbourne, Australia.

Habib is married to **Zakia**.

Mehboob lives in Aziz Bagh, Hyderabad and is married to **Safura.**

Safi , their third son migrated to Australia in December 2005 and completed his education in Business. He is currently working in Melbourne, Australia.
Omar, the youngest in the family is pursuing his intermediate education in Hyderabad.

Mohammed Zafarullah is the youngest of the Valiullah/ Vahidunissa Begum's children.

Upon completing his Bachelor's degree in Science from Osmania University, he proceeded to the United States and obtained Bachelor's degree in Mechanical Engineering from University of Minnesota in 1973. He returned back to Hyderabad, India to spend some time with his parents before migrating to Toronto, Canada in May 1974. He obtained his Master's degree in Management Science from University of Waterloo, Canada in May 1990 while working at Nortel Networks.

Over the past 30 plus years, Zafarullah has executed strategic assignments with major Organizations in Canada, United States and the Asia Pacific Region covering Hong Kong, China, Japan, Korea, Taiwan, Singapore, Thailand, Malaysia, Philippines, Indonesia, Australia, India and Pakistan.

He has held a number of key positions in a variety of functions, including Regional Quality Management/ Compliance, Training, Engineering, New Product Introductions, Project Management, etc.

Until recently, he was based in Hong Kong working for Nortel Networks, and was instrumental in leading key strategic quality and project management initiatives that covered the entire Asia Pacific Region. He had the opportunity to travel extensively in the Asia Pacific Region, and spend time with family members during his visits to India and Pakistan.

His social activities include playing, chess, tennis and table tennis. He won several chess tournaments while representing his school, college and University in India. He led the Osmania University chess team at the All-India inter-university chess tournaments for two consecutive years.

He is a certified Project Management Professional (PMP) with membership in the Project Management Institute, USA, and is currently involved in Management Consulting work based in Chicago.

Mohammed Zafarullah is married to **Tabasum** (daughter of Tasneem Ghias), and they have two daughters: Faaiza and Sameera.
Note: Tasneem Ghias is the granddaughter of Ismatunissa Begum, the maternal aunt of Vahidunissa Begum.

Faaiza is married to Azeemuddin Ahmed, M.D., and they have one daughter: Issma.
Sameera is married to Ali Imran Ahmed, Patent Attorney-At-Law, and they have one son: Momin.

Shamsuddin Ahmed and Mohammed Zafarullah, 2002.

Left, Mohammed Zafarullah and Zaheer Ahmed 1961, and Right, Mohammed Azhar Siddiqui, Mohammed Zafarullah and Zaheer Ahmed several years later.

1936 Ford V8 Convertible was originally owned by Mohammed Valiullah, and was later acquired by Shamsuddin Ahmed.
This picture is from the Annual Vantage Automobile Rally in 1995

The sixth daughter of Aziz Jung

Imtiazunissa Begum married Yousufuddin Ahmed, an educator and Superintendent Excise.

Imtiazunissa Begum and Yousufuddin Ahmed.

Yousufuddin Ahmed was the son of Tajuddin Mohammed. He was a college graduate. He spent his entire life as a very hard working and dedicated and family oriented individual. He had two brothers Sirajuddin Ahmed and Ziauddin Ahmed.

Imtiazunissa Begum and Yousufuddin Ahmed.

Personally, he was a very loving father to all of his children and grandchildren. He always encouraged strong relationships between his own children and their extended relatives.

Earlier in his life he spent some years in the education department. Later on he joined the Central Excise Department and served as Excise Superintendent until he retired.

When their children reached college age, Imtiazunissa begum moved to Aziz Bagh, and Yousufuddin Ahmed stayed by himself during his postings. He was very principled, dedicated personally and professionally.

Yousufuddin spent his last the last thirteen plus years in Chicago, and did not spend his time idly. He was constantly looking for work even at in his later 60s, and finally landed a job at the Palmer House in downtown, and he thoroughly enjoyed his routine every day.

He also discovered a Senior Center in Lombard and used to go there for the social lunch hour every weekday just before departing for work. So he kept himself quite busy from 11:30 am through midnight every day, and loved it.
Back in 1981, Yousufuddin Ahmed became a huge CUBS fan, and influenced his children in their loyalty to the CUBS as well.

They have one daughter and three sons:

Suraiya is married to Dr. Fakruddin Khan, M.D.DCH.FICA. Dr. Fakruddin Khan was professor of pediatrics for 37 years. He was superintendent of Niloufer Hospital. He retired as additional director of medical services. He was professor emiratus at Deccan Medical College. They have four daughters: Kishwar, Kausar, Nayyar, and Niloufer.

Dr. Fakruddin Khan and Suraiya.

Kishwar is married to Mohammed S. Khan (Sajid) who is a mechanical engineer, and they have three children: Sabeen, Saif, and Saba. Sabeen is married to Dr. Masood Ahmed Siddiqui, and they have twins: Usman and Imaan.

Standing Left to Right: Nayyar, Kausar, Farzana, Nilufer, Shahida and Nahid.
Sitting Left to Right: Kishwar, Zarina, Nida. 1969.

Kausar is married to Dr. Ahmed Kamal PhD, and they have three children: Nihal, Zeeshan, and Saniya.

Nayyar is married to Dr. Mohammed Syed (Zia), and they have two sons: Adil and Amer.

Niloufer is married to Dr. Akil Moinuddin, and they have four children: Omar, Hamza, Hiba, and Hana.

Habib U. Ahmed (Rauf) is married to Nasreen daughter of Ahmeduddin and Razia Siddiqui. They have two children: Ali and Yasmeen

Dr. Ali Ahmed is married to Dr. Huma Ahmed and they have four children: Imaan, Zaid, Adil, and Yousuf.

Dr. Yasmeen Ahmed is married to Murtuza Sitabkhan. They have three sons: Zain, Adam, and Riaz.

Dr. Aziz U. Ahmed (Amjad), married to Dr. Nafees. They have five children: Asma, Najma, Uzma, Fatima, and Salma.

Asma is married to Azam Nizamuddin, J.D. They have three sons and one daughter: Nadeem, Fareed, Rasheed, and Asiya.

Dr. Najma is married to Dr. Arshad Papa. They have three children: Mariam, Janna, and Musa.

Dr. Uzma is married to Dr. Omar Hussain. They have two daughters: Noor and Rania.

Dr. Fatima is married to Dr. Ilyas.

Salma is a medical student.

Anees U. Ahmed is married to Zeba. They have two children: Erum and Yousuf (Danish).

Zaheer Ahmed, Mohammed Azhar Siddiqui and Anees Ahmed, 1968.

Anees Ahmed's family drawn by his daughter Erum Ahmed, August 22, 2009

Yousuf Ahmed (Danish), Anees U. Ahmed, Zeba Ahmed and the artist Erum Ahmed.

The Seventh daughter of Aziz Jung

Ismathunissa Begum was known for her mild manners and quite accommodative with all families of Aziz Bagh. She died in December 1975. She was married to Mohammed Yousuf Hussain, BA BT. He started his career as a teacher and retired as a school. He was a man of principles and was s strict disciplinarian. He devoted his retired life in studying Islamic literature. He died in November 1993.

They have three sons and three daughters, one of the daughters Nafees passed away at a very early age.

Siraj, (also known as Zehra) BA, B.Ed. is married to Dr. Hafeezuddin. She retired as teacher and passed away in 1990. They have two daughters and one son.

Dr. Anjum is a Gynocologist and is married to Surgeon Dr. Akbar Hussain. They have two sons and three daughters, Shoeb, B.Com, Umar, Nida, Hana, and Zoya.

Afshan, M.Sc. is married to Mohammed Fareed. They have two daughters, Sana, Arshi and a son Razi.

Azam, B.E, MBA is married to Ayesha Shaeema, B.Sc, B,Ed. They have three sons, Suhaib, Muaz, Mus'ab, and one daughter Asmazehra.

Mohammed Hussain Qureshi B.Com, LL.M (his pen name is Aziz Qureshi) is married to Nafees Fatima, daughter of Gulam Mustafa Chida. Aziz Qureshi was a professor and a scholar of Islamic Jurisprudence and an eminent Urdu Poet. He has taught on Islamic and English Jurisprudence for 20 years in a law college in Karachi. He had been an examiner of Law for Punjab University and Karachi University. He was also accredited examiner of Jurisprudence for Federal Public Service Commission in Islamabad Commission. He has three published books on Jurisprudence in English and five poetry books (Anthologies) in Urdu. Aziz Qureshi is well known in literary circles in America and has been actively participating in local and International Mushairahs in America. He participated in International Urdu conference once in Canada and then in Chicago and read a paper. He was also privileged to represent Urdu writers and poets from America in an International Urdu Seminar in London and presided over a session and read paper.

Bahadur Yar Jung Academy, Karachi. On the occasion of Inaugural function for Aziz Qureshi's 4th poetry collection.

During his thirteen years stay in Abu Dhabi, UAE, he travelled officially to Pakistan, India, Thailand, Singapore, Sri Lanka, Malaysia, Hong Kong, China, Bahrain, Qatar, Saudi Arabia (twice to Hajj), France, Italy, U.K. and USA.

They have three daughters, Asfia, Arshia and Farisa.

Asfia, B.Sc. is married to Zafar Shaffi. They have one son and two daughters. Amir B.S. (Criminal Law). Tania is a college student, and Sania is a student as well.

Arshia, B.A. is married to Syed Iftekhar Quadri. They have one son and one daughter. Wahid B.S. (Marketing) and Mariam is a college student.

Farisa, M.A. is married to Ayaz Nasir. They have one daughter ASyesha and one son Saad, both students.

Mohammed Mushtaq Hussain, B.Sc., B.E. a Civil Engineer M.A., B.Ed. He retired as a lecturer from Osmania University Engineering College. Later he joined Sultan Qaboos University Oman, and worked as a Laboratory Technician and returned to Hyderabad after serving a tenured job. He is married to Nickhat, who worked as lecturer in a college till her retirement.

They have three daughters, Sumaira, Shireen, and Tanveer.

Sumaira, BSc, BS, is married to Mehson Syed Hashim. They have two sons, Umar and Osman.

Shireen, B.Pharm, MBA is married to Mukarram. They have two daughters, Shaizeen and Zaina.

Tanveer, BA, MBA, is married to Moin Faizal. They have two sons Faiz and Danish.

Dr. Mohammed Hamid Hussain, O.B.E. (Order of British Empire), is married to Judith. They have one son Asif and one daughter Robina.

A charismatic and energetic physician, Dr Mohammed Hamid Husain practices in the United Kingdom and is known for his medico-political work, his charitable efforts and his services to medicine and the community. Born in Hyderabad, India, Dr Husain completed his MBBS at Osmania University. He came to the United Kingdom in 1962 and received his early post-graduate training at the Glasgow Royal Infirmary. He subsequently obtained his membership in the Royal College of Physicians of Glasgow, as well as a Fellowship appointment.

He has chaired important medical committees at the local, regional and national level and has sat on the council and on the General Medical Services Committee of the BMA for a number of years. As Chairman of the Organization Committee, Dr Husain steered through the new reformist Constitution of the BMA to introduce more democracy. Over the past 15 years, he has been a member of the panel of appointed Persons of the Medical Advisory Committee. He also serves as an adviser and external assessor to the health service commissioner in England. In 1980, Dr. Husain became the first person to receive a Certificate of Commendation from the British Medical Association in recognition of his outstanding services to the profession; he was subsequently elected as Fellow of the BMA in 1984. In the late 1970's, Dr. Husain campaigned for a No Strike Agreement for the health profession and was invited to address the Social Services Committee at the House of Commons on a new deal for the health service staff to obviate the necessity of industrial action by any group.

Dr. Husain has had a number of articles published in medical journals; he was the first person to describe the presence of Herpes Simplex Virus on Eczematous Skin and identified and described the first person in the United Kingdom to develop rare earth pneumoconiosis. A champion of many charitable causes, Dr. Husain has initiated many campaigns and projects to increase the provision of services for the aged, the disabled and the handicapped for the past 30 years. He was admitted to the Freedom of the Worshipful Society of Apothecaries of the City of London in 1989 and was made a Freeman of the City of London the same year. In 1990, he stepped down from his medico-political activities in order to concentrate on his campaign to raise £2m to establish the world's first Interdisciplinary Research Center dedicated to Multiple Sclerosis, which now forms part of the MRC Cambridge for the Brain Repair.

In recognition of his services to the community and for his charitable work, Rotary International awarded Dr. Husain the Paul Harris Fellowship Medal in 1994. In 1995 he was appointed as an Officer of the most Excellent Order of the British Empire in acknowledgement of his service to medicine. Three years later, the Metropolitan Borough of Rotherham conferred upon him the highest honors it could bestow by making him a Freeman of the Rotherham Borough.

His interests include playing chess, watching cricket, listening to Schubert, reading political biographies and an appreciation of classical art. He and his wife, Judith, a Laboratory Scientist, have two children, Asif and Robina, each of whom holds a Master's Degree from Oxford.

Robina was surrounded with art, music and literature from early childhood. She became an accomplished pianist and performed on television. She also had a flair for singing and dancing. She was an avid reader, a prolific artist, and learnt to speak several languages. Having graduated from the University of Oxford (Jesus College) in French and Spanish, Robina went on to study law and was called to the Bar at Lincoln's Inn. She has worked in the field of European Human Rights law and International Humanitarian Law. Robina's interest in working in humanitarian field saw her undertake two further masters degrees. She obtained a masters in Criminal Justice from the Scarman Centre, Department of Criminology at the University of Leicester, writing her thesis on restorative justice and truth commissions. She obtained a masters degree in Psychotherapy from New School accredited by the University of Sheffield.

Judith, her mother, is renown for her artistic flair, ample expression of which is to be observed throughout their home, Barbot Hall. Together, Robina and Judith started an art business called Sacred Butterflies. Having spotted the commercial viability of Judith's watercolour paintings and Robina's pencil drawings, they now design greetings cards under the company name. Robina continues her dancing and has even done some acting. She appears in the forthcoming Bollywood film 'Veer' with Salman Khan due for release in late 2009.

Asif Husain-Naviatti is a graduate of Oxford University (Christ Church), where he was awarded a scholarship and won the Clifford Smith prize as an undergraduate; Columbia University in New York, where he was a Fulbright Scholar; and he also studied at the University of Vienna as an Erasmus Scholar. He also studied the piano at the Royal Academy of Music in London, and performed in many concerts as a child, including a 1983 concert tour of Japan. He was awarded a limited edition full size concert grand piano by the German piano making company, Grotrian-Steinweg, the parent company of Steinway and Sons. For his post graduate research work in Musicology at Oxford University, he reconstructed Mendelssohn's Second Symphony as it was first performed at its debut in Leipzig. For this, he was awarded an M.Litt.

He has been an international civil servant, primarily with the United Nations, since 1994, and has worked in London, New York, Washington DC, Haiti, Kosovo, Sierra Leone and Iraq, and has traveled to many other countries during the course of his professional assignments. He has served as Advisor on AIDS to the Secretary-General of the United Nations, Kofi Annan, in which role he guided the Secretary-General's high-level advocacy strategy contributing to a sea-change in the global fight against AIDS. He is currently working on the reconstruction and development of Iraq, as a staff member of the United Nations Development Programme (UNDP). He opened the first UNDP offices in Kurdistan and Baghdad since the 2003 evacuation.

In December 2009, he will marry Ms ShiMin Chen, providing the family's first marital link with China.

Rafath Fatima is married to Masood Mohiuddin, B.E. a Civil Engineer, was a lecturer in Osmanioa University Engineering College. After retirement he has been working as a lecturer in another Engineering College at Hyderabad. They have two daughters, Tasneem, B.Sc, B.Ed is married to Syed Kazim Hussari. They have one Mazon and one daughter Moha. Tabasum is a student.

The eighth daughter of Aziz Jung

Resource: Mohammed Mohiuddin and Shirlee Walsh

Left: Khurshidunissa Begum, Right: Khurshidunissa Begum with her husband Nasiruddin Khan.

Khurshidunisa Begum was the youngest and the only child of Aziz Jung who migrated to Pakistan. She died in Karachi in 1995.

KHURSHEDD UN NISA AND FAMILY
Born 8 Rajab - Died 14th Jamadiul Awal (October 16, 1995).

- Youngest daughter of AZIZ JUNG
- Married to NAWAB MUHAMMAD NASEERUDDIN KHAN son of NAWAB SADIQ JUNG BAHADUR
- In the start lived in India and then left everything and came to Pakistan
- She was very humble and polite and was loving in nature
- She was a good poet and her TAKALUS was KANEEZ
- Her poetry was mostly about Prophet Muhammad PBUH
- She like Persian and said some poems in Persian too.
- She liked to read books on faith and religion
- She had no interest in the lime lights of the world
- She was simple and use to left everything on Allah's will
- She was a women of many talents, including cooking , sewing and embroidery
- Her will power was on very high level which helped her face the difficulties of the world
- She live a very struggling life but never complained to anyone
- She was kind hearted and gave to other people with an open heart and hand
- She was willing to sacrifice everything to help others

Khursheedunissa's daughters and son:

1. **ALIA JAMAL** married to late Mirza Salahuddin
One son Dr. Mehboob Mirza, married to Dr. Hina Naseem, they have three daughters. One daughter Nazia Haseeb married to Haseeb Saied who is a banker. They have three daughters, late Nabia Haseeb, Second daughter Samia Haseeb, studying to become a Pharmacist, and Areeba Haseeb.

2. **SIDDIQA JAMAL** married to late Saieduddin Siddiqui, he was a banker. They have two sons and two daughters, Haseeb Saied married to Nazia Haseeb.

Fauzia M. Hafeez married to Syed Mateem Hafeez a Pharmacist. They have three Sons. Ayaz Hafeez a Lawer is married to Huma Hosain who is a medical student, Faraz Hafeez, also a medical student and Moiz Hafeez.

Ahmed Mujeeb Siddiqui, a Pharmacist is married to Ambreen Mujeeb. They have two daughters and one son, Wajeeha Siddiqui, Hafsah Siddiqui, and Riyan Ahmed Siddiqui.

Moina Sajjad is married to Sajjad Hasan, he is an Engineer. They have three daughters. Khadijah Sajjad, Mahibah Sajjad, and Mariam Sajjad

3. **FARIDA SHAIDA** married to late Asif Shaida, they have two sons and two daughters.

4.**NASIR MOHIUDIN** is married to Shirlee Walsh

5. **SABIHA MUNEER** is married to Muneer Safvi who is a Marketing Manager. They have one Daughter Dr. Sana Muneer who is married to Rashid who is an engineer. They have one daughter Alaina.

6. **TAYABBA SAHREEF** is married to Shareef-ul-Hasan who is a retired teacher. They have four sons and two daughters

7. **MASOOMA ASEEM** is married to Syed Muhammed Aseem a banker. They have one son one daughter, Dr. Syed Muhammed Tauseef Faisal and Dr. Asma Hasan.

Chapter 8

Biography of Dr. Hasanuddin Ahmed, I.A.S and Anees H. Ahmed

Dr. Hasanuddin Ahmed, IAS.

Dr. Hasanuddin Ahmed is the son of Deen Yar Jung and the grandson of Aziz Jung. He is a member of the Indian Administrative Service and is known for his has outstanding administrative and scholastic abilities.

He married to Anees Fatima on 1st May 1947. Anees Fatima is a very talented lady. She is a certified teacher with a B.A., B. Ed degree. After teaching at Mahboobia Girls' School briefly, she began a long career serving the community.

Dr. and Mrs. Hasanuddin Ahmed in 1947 on left, and in 1972 right.

Anees Fatima was the General Secretary of the ICSW, (Indian Council of Social Works). She was Commissioner of Girl's Guide. She is well travelled person, having visited every continent except the Antarctica. As a young girl, she actively participated in sports with her favorite cousin, Ruqhia. All members of the family look upon her as their mentor and advisor. She is a tireless woman who has always been interested in serving the community.

Dr. Hasanuddin Ahmed as a youth was very serious about his studies. He was aware of the burden he was expected to carry being the descendent of a highly qualified family of noble members. While still young, he organized the 'Bazme Iqbal' and celebrated 'Iqbal Day'. He founded 'Villa Academy Publication, which has published sixty-two books, including previously un published works by Aziz Jung as well as other scholars.

Dr. Hasanuddin Ahmed was an officer of the Indian Administrative Services, the Ex-Chairman of the Minorities Commission, and the Ex-Chairman of the Andhra Pradesh State Wakf Board, along with being a scholar and author.

Dr. Hasanuddin Ahmed in his office, 1972.

His books include 'Nature Cure' and the Urdu translation of 'Srimad Bhagavath Gita' which he completed while he was still a student. The 'Urdu Word Count' was his magnum opus (lifetime great contribution), which is a useful resource to Urdu scholars throughout the world. 'An Easy Way to the Understanding of the Qur'an', published in the United States by the Iqra International Publishers, is a noteworthy book on the Qur'an. His other books, 'A New Approach to the Understanding of the Qur'an', and 'Ulmul Qur'an', were published by Goodword Book, New Delhi. His most recent book, 'History of the Muslim Ummah', was recently published.

Two of his books were released by the then Prime Minister of India Indira Gandhi, two by the then President of India Fakhruddin Ali Ahmed, and two by Sardar Surjeet Singh Barnala as Governor of Andhra Pradesh and as Governor of Tamilnadu, respectively.

Clockwise from left: Governor Ali Yaver Jung, Dr. Hasanuddin Armed, Dr. Hasanuddin Ahmed with President of India, Fakhruddin Ali Ahmed and the first lady Abida Ahmed Begum and Anees H. Ahmed.

In 1954 he attended the World Pacifist Conference and the World Religion Congress in Japan. He started the 'Pustak Daan' movement where Urdu books were donated to foreign countries to promote Urdu. He started libraries in Japan, Czechoslovakia, Israel, and Russia.

He is responsible for the construction of Ghalib Hall in the Mehboobnagar district of Andhra Pradesh. While he was still at Mehboobnagar he founded a school for the poor, which was run by the officer's wives. Today the school is funded by the government and has full time teachers.

Dr. Ahmed was the President of the Indo-Middle East Cultural Studies, Founder/President of the Villa Academy and General Secretary of the All India Amir Khusrau Society whose Presidents included the President of India Fakhruddin Ali Ahmed and later Governor Ali Yaver Jung.

Dr. Ahmed spent almost thirty-six years serving the State and Central Governments occupying responsible positions. In the year 1973, while in New Delhi, his book 'Urdu Word Count' was released by the Prime Minister of India, Indira Gandhi, at her residence. It was presented to her by I. K. Gujral who was the Cabinet Minister of Information and Broadcasting.

Prime Minister of India Indira Gandhi releasing Dr. Hasanuddin Ahmed's book presented by Brahamanand Reddy.

Another book by Dr. Ahmed was released in New Delhi by President Fakhruddin Ali Ahmed. This book was called, 'Life, Time and Works of Amir Khusrau Dehlavi'. The book was the product of Dr. Ahmed's dedication and scholastic abilities.

1980, Dr. Ahmed founded the Amir Khusrau Society of North America in Chicago and Toronto. Dr. Hasanuddin Ahmed appointed Dr. Habib Ahmed as President of the Amir Khusrau Society of America for the Chicago Chapter. In 1987 Iqra Publications International published 'An Easy Way to the Understanding of the Qur'an'. This book was very highly acclaimed worldwide, and was later translated from English into several languages including Urdu, Telugu, and Hindi. Dr. Ahmed was invited to Pakistan when the revised Urdu edition was released.

He also served as Member of the Central Wakf Council. He was the Chairman Minorities Commission, with State Minister's rank.

Left: The mayor of Rotherham, UK presenting an honorary plaque to Dr. Hasanuddin Ahmed.
Right: Dr. Hamid Hussain, OBE., Anees H. Ahmed, Zehra Hyder, Aziz Ahmed, and Judith Hussain, 2006.

Dr. Hasanuddin Ahmed
with Prince Muffakham Jah,
grandson of the Nizam VII.

Chapter 9

Memoirs – Razia Siddiqui
Contributed by Farhana Zia

A letter to Razia Fatima Siddiqui

Meri Ma,
I look out the window and Boston Harbor looms ahead. You, I have just left behind, your beautiful frame silhouetted in soft sheets, your voice frail, your eyes filled with now ever present sleep. *Khuda Hafiz, Meri Bacchi*, you say. When will I see you again?

I don't want to go. I don't want to leave you, Meri Ma.

Back in my home I stare at you, locked on my wall, framed by the halo of beauty and youthful expectation. You took over the helm much too soon and you steered and navigated our small ship with such strength, wisdom and fortitude. How did you do it?

What do I really know of you? I know so little of your selfless giving—so little of the many differences you made in a myriad lives. How does one attain what you attained? How is it possible to give so much from such a bottomless reservoir of giving? How is it possible to command such universal respect and admiration? How did you do it all?

You gave so much but now you are reluctant to take.
How long? you ask. *How long will she keep doing for me*?
Your asking pierces my heart. How shall I answer you, Meri Ma?
Perhaps it's your time to be on the other end of the giving now. The giver gives with such uncompromising grace. I wish I could do what she does with so much love, fortitude and good humor always shining in her silvery laugh.

But all I do from a distance is pray that you continue to endure with your quiet patience and steely strength.

I love you, Meri Ma,
Farhana

Memoirs – Razia Siddiqui
Contributed by Mohammed Azher Siddiqui

Dear Mamma,

Seventeen months ago, I penned a few words to commemorate the 45th anniversary of Dad's passing away. With this note, I want to celebrate your 84th birthday in July and pay tribute to your life. And what a life it has been. Through you, I have glimpsed those ancestors I never met. Your stories made both your grandmothers practically come alive before me. Your description of how Baba (Nawab Deen Yar Jung) used to say "*Salam araz karta hoon*" from behind a curtain to his mother-in-law and her response of "*Jeete Raho, Allah umar daraz kare*" made it seem like I was a personal witness to that era. Your narration of how proud you felt when Baba asked you to bring him a glass of water when you were already married and a mother of three, so eloquently describes the love and respect you had for him. Another recollection brings alive your early family life with the requisite discipline as well as unconditional love. It's the time when Baba's injunction was that only the two oldest children would be able to get in the car for a family outing. Seeing the disappointment on your face, Aga (Janab Hasanuddin Ahmad) took your hand and pulled you inside the car. Once in, you both nervously glanced at your father, only to see him turn away as the slightest of smiles gained visibility on his face.

I never actually saw Amanna (Begum Azhar Jung Bahadur) walk. My earliest memories of her have always been running the entire family from her "*takhat*" in Azher Mansion. It is again through your narrations, that I know her as a vibrant woman who kept the entire Azhar Jung family running like clockwork.

My love for our Prophet developed at a very early age because of your narration of the Hadiths to us as children. When faced by a dilemma, I remember you wondering how he would have addressed the situation. No man can aspire to even think about how he would have addressed any situation. However, just the thought that he faced so many unimaginably complex problems, always provided comfort and made our issues du-jour, seem so miniscule.

At an early age you instilled a high level of confidence in your children. I remember arguing that traveling from Rajkot to Surat and changing trains there for Bombay was just a tad too difficult for an eight year old. I wanted you to come from Calcutta to Rajkot to fetch me for summer vacations. Perhaps it was Dad, but you were the deliverer of the message that I could, and should do it. I still remember the feeling of profound relief when I used to spot you in the crowded Bombay Central station. I also remember making you pay the price of my solitary adventure travel all through the two day ride from Bombay to Calcutta. The bitterness and anger would dissipate by the time Dad came to receive us at Howrah. The rest of the Siddiqui family enjoyed my angelic side, while you bore the brunt of the devilish one.

After Dad's passing, you took control of the family. In a short span of 14 years you oversaw school and college graduations and three marriages. As if this was not enough, on the side, you built the new Azhar Mansion, fenced the "Lake View" property, had a well dug for our Gandipait farm and supervised the building of the new veranda in Aziz Bagh. My fanaticism about working out, climbing mountains and traversing deserts is a directly inherited trait! That, and Dada Hazrath's (Azhar Jung Bahadur) legendary prowess with the "*mukhdars*"*!*

Your coming to the United States in the mid 70's, learning to drive and working not one but two jobs, all the while helping to run a house with two very boisterous children, was a spectacular achievement. The twenty plus years you and Daisy spent living under the same roof, with genuine love and respect for each other is an example of how an in-law relationship should be. Having worked two jobs from 1979 to 1999 you could have saved a lot of money; instead you gave it all away before moving to Chicago. Many a house has been built and many a family found their feet because of your personal commitment and generosity.

When faced with a choice of doing the right thing or doing the profitable thing, you always taught us to do the right thing as ultimately that would also prove to be profitable. That advice has come true for me more times than I can count. In a world replete with daily compromises on culture, morals, upbringing and beliefs all in the effort to "fit" in, you showed us by example that there is only black and white in core beliefs. There are no compromises, no shades of grey. Doing the right thing has indeed turned out, for me, to be very profitable. Daisy and I have passed your message on to Raza and Laila that we are the ambassadors of our family, our culture and our religion.

Even now, when Apa (Nasreen Ahmed) takes you for your dialysis and when one can plainly see your weakened physical condition, you have proven that the power of the mind is so much greater than that of the body. Earlier this year, when I took you inside the dialysis room, you called over Lenny, your male nurse from Philippines and said something in his native tongue. Having received Lenny's enthusiastic handshake it was obvious that I had just been introduced as your son from Boston. Goal setting has always been your forte. Today, you are a living example of one who has now taken up learning Filipino as your next challenge.

At the end of the day, everyone needs to take stock of the life they have led. If they have no regrets, it is a life well lived. I would think anyone would be envious of the life you have lived as a grandchild, a daughter, a sibling, a wife, a mother, a grandmother and now a great-grand mother. The fact that all your descendants care so much about you and want to be with you, speaks volumes.

President Reagan summed up his years in the White House by saying "My friends we did it. We weren't just marking time. We made a difference. We made the city stronger. We made the city freer and we left her in good hands. All in all, not bad, not bad at all". I think you can very well say the same. After leaving the White House, he lived an additional sixteen years with the well wishes and prayers of people whose hearts and minds he had touched. I know you have touched and enriched many lives and we all know that you have their prayers and well wishes. May the rest of your years be full of family and hugs and may laughter ring around you. These are the things that make life rich. For you, I will add another wish – may the Indian T.V serial *"Teen Bahuraniyan*" continue and may the Gorodia family also find happiness!

On July 23rd, I will be away in Mongolia (Insha Allah), chasing the solar eclipse across the Gobi desert, but my thoughts and prayers will continue to be with you as you blow out 83 candles.

Respectfully,

Mohammed Azher Siddiqui

Memoirs – Ahmeduddin Siddiqui
Contributed by Farhana Zia

Dearest dad,

Apa has put together an album that has become my best treasure. It's a beautiful testimony of the life you made possible for us. The small black and white stills chronicle family and family moments and capture with utter brilliance the essence of our happy life and its myriad moments of bliss. For that charmed life, Dad, we still thank you.

Ahmeduddin Siddiqui, Razia Siddiqui,
Nasreen, Farhana and Mohammed Azher Siddiqui.

Mummy saw sixteen glorious years beside you; Apa had fifteen years; I had thirteen, and ten. Hardly enough time with you, by anybody's reckoning but what a rich a life it was and what wealth of happy memories we have of it! Forty-five years ago that life ended for us. The image of the lorry carrying you away is vivid and the sound of Mummy's broken bangles still thunders in my ears. I had intended to wake up to the next morning to find you well and healthy but around 1'oclock in the morning, you left with a quiet apology. We wished you were with us. We missed you more than you could know. We wanted you at school graduations and marriages and childbirths. We needed you to steer, to advice and to comfort. We wanted you, very selfishly, all for us.

Your children have surpassed you in years now. Apa and I are mothers and grandmothers and Azher's son, Raza, married last month. Decades have passed but you are still rooted firmly in our hearts and we look for a little bit of your excellence to percolate down and find us. Even now you are the greatest love of Mummy's life, her noble prince, her ideal man. Even today I feel blessed that you were my father, as do Apa and Azher.

I love you,
Your daughter
Farhana

Memoirs – Ahmeduddin Siddiqui
Contributed by Mohammed Azher Siddiqui

Dear Dad,
There are times when I miss not having you around, even now 45 years to the day after your passing. One such time was on November 17th 2006 when Raza got married. It would have given you great pleasure to see how well all your grandchildren have turned out and how they are making their way in today's world, straddling two cultures.

Ahmeduddin Siddiqui, Razia Siddiqui, Nasreen, Farhana, and Mohammed Azher Siddiqui.

Having said that I miss you, I also have to say that I see your presence and personality shine through your descendants. I look at Nasreen and see the stoicism and resolution that I know she inherits from you and mom. I see Farhana, and as Daisy has said time and again, "Farhana is the model of decency". I know these traits come from you. I see Ali and the wonderful way he interacts with his elders and the genuine compassion, care and love he shows towards his extended family and I know he inherits it from you. I know Omar gets his caring nature from you.

I have always told my children that everyone falls; the difference is who gets up the quickest, brushes off the dust and resumes the race. I have to say Raza is an epitome of overcoming obstacles. In a culture that venerates certain professions, both Raza and Laila have blazed a trail of their own. Into uncharted territories they have delved, fearless and head-on, and made a success of their young professional lives. I am sure they inherit this from you. I can only imagine how hard it must have been for you to have passed Hyderabad Civil Service (HCS) with flying colors receiving the Sir Akbar Hyderi Gold medal, only to see your world turned upside down with the State of Hyderabad being taken over by the Republic of India. You adapted to the changes and shone as the brightest star in the Indian Administrative Service, later transferring to Indian Accounts and Audit Services, keeping intact your culture, values and religion while forging ahead in the new republic. You sir, did everything with class.

Raza's understated sense of humor is definitely yours. Laila's single-minded focus and dedication to any task at hand is a directly inherited trait. Her compassion, empathy for the less fortunate, and high regard for social work has resulted in her becoming a volunteer fire fighter and EMT. She does this without complaint or fanfare, all the while holding a challenging full time job. I see you and Laila's maternal grandfather, Mahmood Ali, in her everyday. Her values, especially those related to Zakat, she inherits from her beloved "Amma", Razia Fatima.

Finally I look to myself. I have been to 32 countries in five continents and seen every state (except Alaska) at least twice, and yet I will fly to the 33rd country on a moments notice and with the greatest of joy. This love of travel, I know I inherit from both my parents. I remember how happy you were to go to Nepal when we were small tots and I remember the polished stones you picked up from the foothills of the Himalayas to bring back to us. I remember how you and Mom just took off on a whim for Delhi leaving us with Moni and Kedhu Ram, two of your trusted helpers who, like many others, would do anything for you.

The summation of one's life is best written or quoted by someone other than immediate family. Let me then quote such a person. In 2005, we went to Chicago to attend a family wedding. Afzal Maama had come from India to attend this function as well. Your name came up during the conversation and I was awed by the love and genuine respect with which he recalled small instances of his remembrance. This from a much younger in-law, who probably met you no more than a time or two - more than 45 years ago! The only true legacy one leaves behind is ones name. You certainly have left us a remarkable one.

Fifty years ago you acknowledged my life by writing an article entitled "My young animal". This small note is an unworthy attempt to celebrate yours.

I still miss you, but when I do, I just look around and find you in your descendants.

Respectfully,

Mohammed A. Siddiqui
12/23/06

Memoirs – Nasreen Ahmed

Contributed by Mohammed Azher Siddiqui

As I make a concerted effort to push aside the fog of memory from a time gone by, a picture of a vibrant little girl in a white dress emerges from the mist. The little girl is full of life and always singing, climbing trees and playing with our dog, Rover. When she is not engaged in outdoor activities, she is practicing *Bharat Natyam* or playing the *sitar*. At dusk, this girl does not leave to go home as our neighbor Munni does. Observing the special affection my father showers on her and combining that with the commands she issues to the two other children in the house, I begin to deduct the concept of an older sibling. The occasional lecture and the frequent smart slaps she would bestow confirmed the fact that she was someone to look up to as well as learn from. Because she ran a tight ship and obviously enjoyed a higher position in the family hierarchy, it was with some pleasure that I would watch her get a dressing-down from my mother when she made a fuss taking her nightly dose of *tonic* that we were all subjected to growing up in Ranchii. These are some of my earliest memories of my sister, Nasreen Ahmed.

In 2006, I wrote a short article celebrating my father Ahmeduddin Siddiqui's life and earlier this year about my mother, Razia Siddiqui in celebration of her 84th birthday. I have had occasion, while sitting at an airport in some corner of world to think about our parents and their legacy and it has focused my thoughts very sharply on Nasreen, or *Apa* as we call her. Apa represents the best combination of the qualities of both my parents. Her stoicism and reserved approach is a reflection of my fathers endearing qualities and her strength of character and strong will, some would call it stubbornness, is directly inherited from our mother.

Some of my other memories are of us growing up in my grandfather Nawab Azhar Jung's household in Hyderabad, where Apa was the apple of my grandmother's eyes. Both our *chacha's*, Moinuddin Sahib and Nizamuddin Sahib doted on her. We did have six older cousins, but they were a generation older than us, so Nasreen, being the eldest of the next set of Nawab Azhar Jung's grandchildren was everyone's darling. I don't know this, but as a child, I am told that my *chacha*, Moinuddin used to take her every night from my mother and walk her in his arms until she fell asleep. This love was returned in full measure. My sister would, at the slightest excuse, hug both our uncles and more often than not we would find her on my grandmother,

Begum Azhar Jung's *takhat,* clipping her toenails, combing her hair, arranging her books or tending to her other needs.

Although a very close-knit family, my sisters and I were not destined to spend much time together as children. I lived with my parents for a short time when my father was stationed in Rajkot and later when he was transferred to Calcutta; my sisters come to live with my parents while I was left behind in a boarding school. When both Nasreen and Farhana were left behind in my other grandfather, Nawab Deen Yar Jung's house, she assumed the responsibility and became a de-facto guardian for her younger sister. The reverential outlook that Farhana has for Nasreen, I am sure was developed in those early formative years.

We were reunited briefly after my fathers passing and once again, Apa assumed her leadership role. I recall one occasion when Farhana and I were burning the midnight oil, while Apa was fast asleep. We heard a faint drone, which very quickly developed into an angry buzz. We looked up to see a swarm of bees honing in on the lamp behind us. The two of us dove into our respective mosquito nets and soon an argument ensued about who should be brave enough to step out and switch off the lamp so that the bees would dissipate. The argument woke Nasreen, who quickly surmised the situation and quietly left the safety of her mosquito net, stepped up to the lamp, reached for the switch amidst a flotilla of bees, switched off the light, returned to her bed and fell asleep while Farhana and I watched in astonishment.

Our time together, albeit short, was fulfilling. Nasreen was married in 1966 and left for the U.S, just as I was really beginning to know her. The letters were frequent, but certainly were no match for physical proximity. Soon my nephew Ali was born in 1967 and that year my other sister got married and also left for the U.S. It was after a long gap of nine years, when Daisy and I got married and I moved to the U.S myself that we picked up on the relationship we had started to develop in the mid- sixties. My mother left India in 1979 and came to live with us in Boston the year our son Raza was born. The 18 years that my mother lived with us and gave us the best years of her life were a true testament to her selflessness. I am especially proud of the fact that my mother and my wife enjoyed a very special bond and lived harmoniously under the same roof. It is not too far a stretch to say that this is not a recurring theme. As a matter of fact, the only other example of such harmonious co-existence, that I have observed, is between Apa and her daughter-in-law Huma. It is heartwarming to see the love, respect, friendship and camaraderie they have for each other.

When my mother's health started failing in the late 90's, Apa sat us down and affirmed that our mother should move to Chicago where she would be under her constant supervision. I am stumped to think of any other person that would take over a parent in failing health, after seeing that parent give their best years to a sibling. Apa, once again proved what many of us already knew about her. As the prophet *(pbuh)* said, if there is a heaven on earth, it is under the mother's feet and Apa certainly has secured that spot.

Looking after our mother is only one of her many tasks. Over the last year, I have had occasion to visit Chicago several times and I am amazed to see how seamlessly Apa performs her chores as a daughter and a care giver, while supervising and schooling her six grandchildren and ensuring that she saves the weekends to spend with her husband. With all this, she still finds time to listen to and advise her nephew Raza. It is not a far stretch to say that she raised Raza, who left Boston at age eighteen to go to college in Illinois. Raza had not learned to drive and my sister used to drive him to his summer school in Joliet from Bolingbrook, wait three hours while he finished his classes and then drive him back to Bolingbrook where she lived then. No wonder then that Raza calls her his other mother.

Every generation has a person who is respected and looked up to. I look at the generation that precedes us and without any hesitation; will give that special title to my *maami,* Begum Hasanuddin Ahmed. When I look at my generation, I unflinchingly bestow this title on my sister Nasreen Ahmed. I set myself goals and timelines and measure my progress on how best I meet these milestones. I look at the compassion, caring, love, respect and unquestioned loyalty that Apa shows to everyone and I honestly have to say that I will not be able to attain her lofty standards. What is even more humbling is that she does all this without any regard to self or any expectations in return.

Over the years, I have spoken to several family members and in one way or another; they have voiced a similar admiration for my sister. Apa celebrates her birthday on November 23rd and the only meaningful present I can give her is to pray that she enjoys a long and healthy life and sees her own family grow, prosper and learn to love one another as she has loved us all. I am sure my extended family will join me in this heart-felt prayer, while wishing her a very happy birthday.

Mohammed Azher Siddiqui.
November 23rd 2008

Chapter 10

Bawarchi Khana, (Recipes)

Aziz Bagh is famous for its unique food. The age old authentic and traditional recipes are well preserved. New recipes are also constantly created. The slogan of the family is, "eat to live, serve humanity and be grateful to God".

Tandoori Chicken

This recipe of mine was published in the 1979 book, 'Potpourri of Cookery', Treasured Publications, Inc. on page 85 in the Poultry section.

Ingredients:
1 lb. Chicken, 1 tsp salt, 2 tbsp lemon juice, 1 tsp coriander powder, 1-1/2 tsp garlic powder, 1 tsp ginger, 1 tsp red hot pepper, 1 tbsp vinegar, 1 tbsp salad or olive oil, 1 cup yogurt.

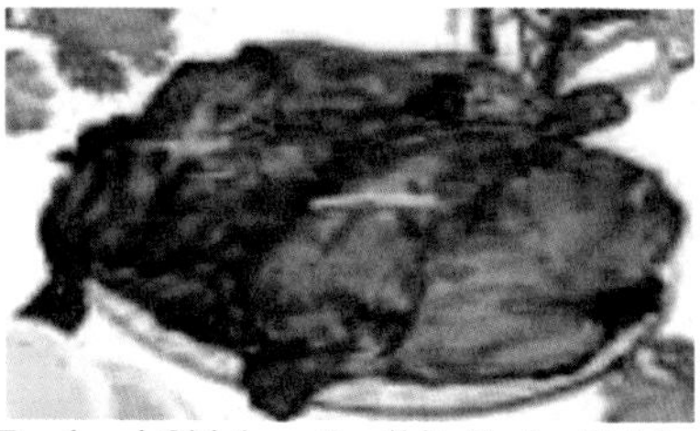

Tandoori Chicken, I call it, 'Luku Chicken'.

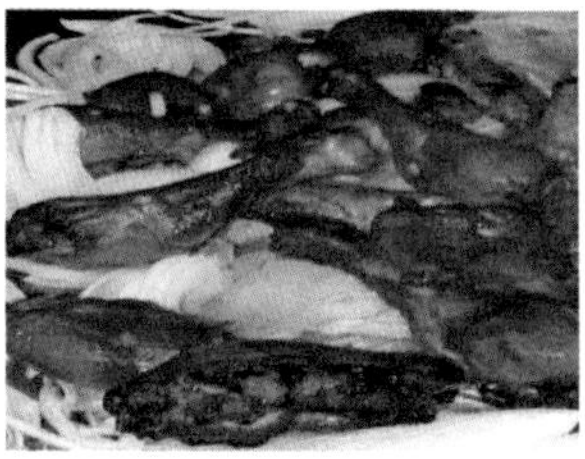

Luku Chicken ready to eat.

Method:
Make slits on the breasts and legs. Rub salt and lemon juice on the chicken. Let stand about 30 minutes. Mix the rest of the ingredients into yogurt, and then marinate the chicken for about 4-6 hours until it is soaked in the paste.

Grill in oven for 45 minutes at 375 degrees until it is crispy brown. Apply butter half way through baking. Add orange color (erythrosine) 5-7 drops.

Serve with onions and fresh lemons.

Roast Venison

Venison (deer meat) is a rare delicacy. The meat is extremely lean and healthy. You will love this recipe. Cooking this delicacy is not nearly as hard as it is to actually find the venison meat.

Also note that this delicacy is not easy to prepare, but in the end, the effort is well worth it. Don't be scared to attempt this gourmet dish.

This is an original recipe of my own, like all my other recipes, but this one took me many years to perfect. The reason is since deer is a wild animal thrives on wild food, the meet is a bit smelly. This is known as game smell. The use of turmeric powder and vinegar takes care of the 'Game Smell'.

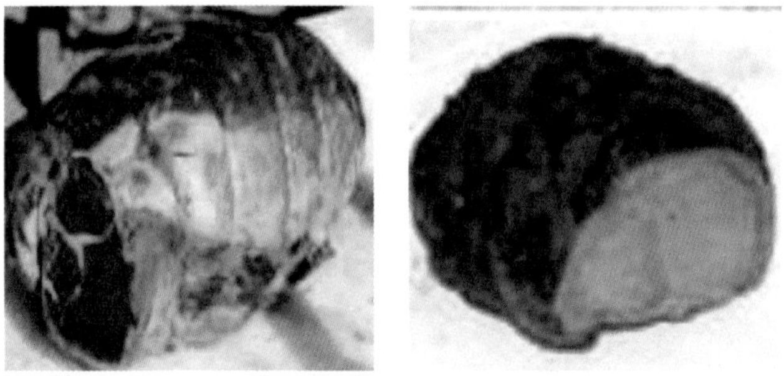

Venison Roast, raw and cooked

Ingredients:
2 lbs Venison Roast.

Stage One Ingredients:
1 cup lemon juice, 1 tsp salt.

Stage Two Ingredients:
1 whole green pepper, hara masala, 1 whole onion. Grind these ingredients in a blender with 1 cup lemon juice.

Stage Three Ingredients:
1 tsp red hot pepper, 2 tsp ginger, 2 tsp garlic, salt to taste, 2 tsp black pepper, and 1 tsp haldi.

Stage Four Ingredients:
1 cup vinegar.

Method:
Clean the Venison Roast in COLD water. Cold water cleaning is absolutely necessary. Do not use even lukewarm water. So cold water it is.

Apply Stage One Ingredients and let it marinate for an hour.

Apply Stage Two Ingredients and let it marinate another one hour.

Apply Stage Three Ingredients and let it marinate one hour.

Sprinkle Stage Four Ingredients (Vinegar) and let it marinate one hour.

Bake the Venison Roast in oven for 45 minutes at 325 degrees temperature.

You are almost done, but not quite ready to eat yet. There is more. Remove the Roast from the oven and fry it in a pan until dark brown.

Suggestion: Eat either straight, or with Malaysian Parata or with regular Hyderabad Deccani Ghee Parata.

Mouth-watering Venison leg roast, ready to eat.

Beef/Lamb/Venison Steaks

Ingredients:

1 lb steak, 1/2 tsp red hot pepper, 1 tsp ginger, 1 tsp garlic, 1 tomato, 1 whole green hot pepper, 1 small onion, salt to taste, 2 tsp coriander seeds, 2-3 tbsp lemon juice, 1 tbsp white vinegar, 1/2 tsp cloves. Add barbecue sauce if desired.

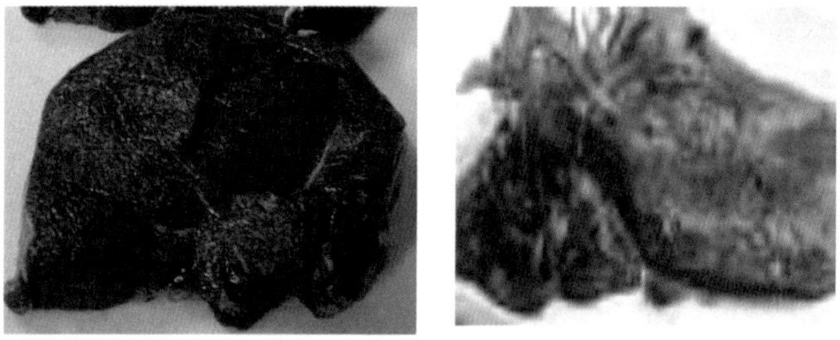

Venison Steak, raw and cooked.

Method:
Mix above ingredients in a blender, and marinate the steak for at least 4-6 hours.

Broil at 375 degrees in the oven or grill until well cooked. I have tried both broiling and grilling. I preferred the grilling.

Beef /Lamb/Venison Ribs

Ingredients:

1 lb ribs, 1/2 tsp red hot pepper, sprinkle some black pepper for flavor, 1 tsp ginger, 1 tsp garlic, 3 tbsp barbecue sauce, 1 whole green hot pepper , 1 small onion, Salt to taste, 1 tsp coriander seeds, 2-3 tbsp lemon juice. barbecue sauce is optional as per your personal preference.

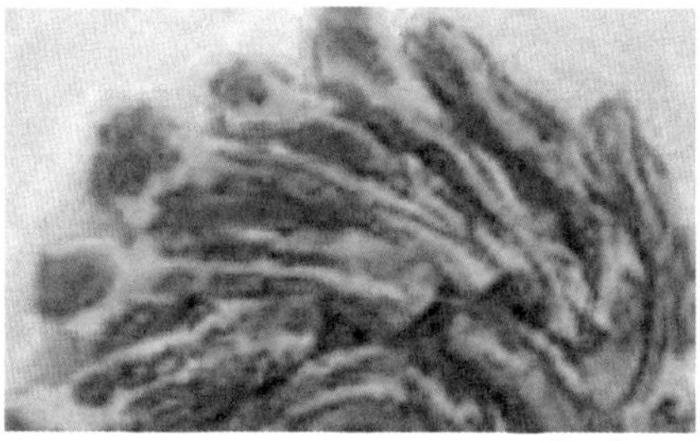
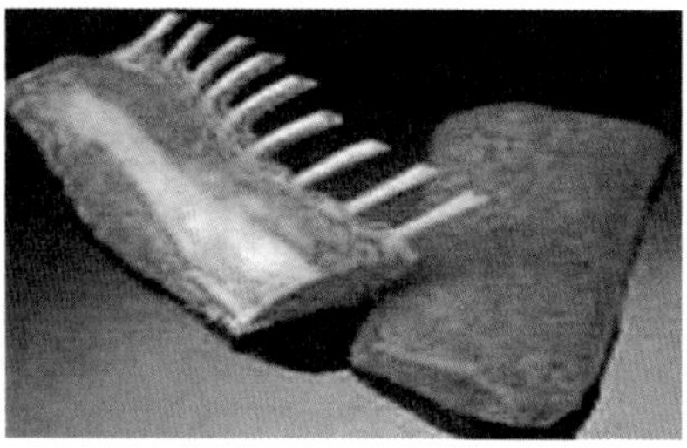
Venison Ribs Raw.

Method:
Mix above ingredients in a blender, and marinate the ribs for at least 6-8 hours.

Broil the ribs in the oven for 35 minutes or until cooked. I have tried both grilling, and broiling. I prefer grilling.

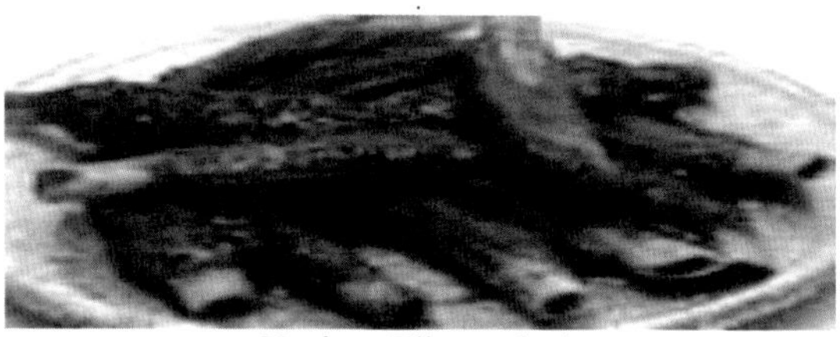
Venison Ribs cooked.

Beef/Lamb/Venison Chops

Ingredients:
1/2 lb chops, 2 tbsp curd or yogurt, 1/2 tsp red hot pepper, 1 tsp ginger, 1 tsp garlic, 1 tomato, 1 whole green hot pepper, 1 small onion, salt to taste, 1 tsp coriander seeds, 2-3 tbsp lemon juice, 2 tsp soy sauce.

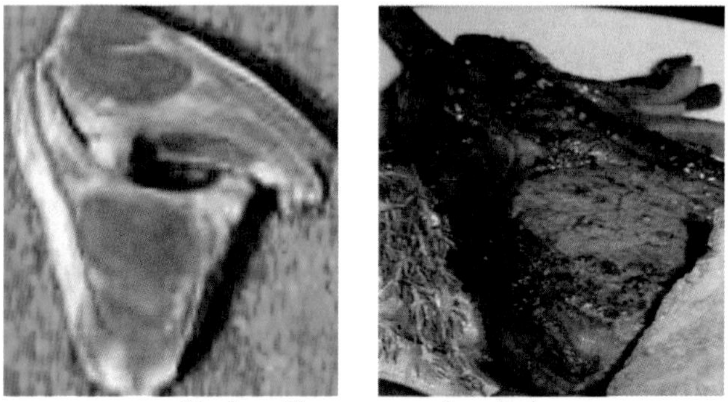

Venison Chops, raw and cooked.

Method:
Mix above ingredients in a blender and marinate the chops for at least 6-8 hours.

Fry the chops on a frying pan until golden brown. I have tried both grilling, and frying but frying is juicer and far superior. The entire house fills with smoke but the taste is unbeatable. Mix ingredients and marinate the chops for at least 4-6 hours.

Fried Shrimps/Prawns

Ingredients:
1 lb shrimp, 1 fresh lemon, 5-6 whole black pepper, 1 tsp turmeric powder, 1/2 chilli powder, 2-3 cut green chilies, 1 tsp coriander powder, 1 tsp cumin powder, 1 small onion, salt to taste, olive oil, water, 2 tsp soy sauce.

Shrimps, raw and cooked.

Method:
Marinate the shrimps with salt, turmeric powder and chili powder. Grind lemon juice and black pepper to fine paste. Fry onions in olive oil and soy sauce until golden brown. Add coriander powder, cumin powder, and shrimps. Fry for a minute and add 1 cup of water, cut green chilies and cover. When shrimps are cooked, serve with garnish coriander leaves and onions.

Potato Baked In Spice

Ingredients:
4 medium potatoes, 2 tsp garlic, 3 tsp ginger, 2-3 tsp chili powder, salt to taste, 4 tsp olive oil, one cup yogurt or sour cream.

Method:
Cut potatoes into 4 pieces each, heat the oil and add the ginger, garlic and chili powder. Fry until light brown, then add salt and half cup of water.

Cover the pan and cook at low temperature until potatoes are cooked and water is evaporated. Add some more oil and cook a little while longer. When done, pour yogurt or sour cream over the potatoes.

I love the end result!

Baked potatoes, raw and cooked.

Lemon Chutney

Ingredients:
1/2 cup fresh lemon juice, 1 1/2 tsp chili powder, 1/4 tsp methi powder, black pepper, salt to taste, 1/2 tsp olive oil, fresh garlic, ginger, and mustard seeds.

Optional:
Some soy sauce and fresh tomatoes may be added for additional flavor.

Method:
Add chili powder, black pepper, garlic, ginger, salt and methi powder to lemon juice. Heat oil and mustard seeds, when the mustard seeds pop add to the spicy lemon juice.

Lemon Chutney, before and after.

Chapter 11

Terms used in this Book

Aziz Bagh: Residence of Aziz Jung's family.

Aziz Jung: Ahmed Abdul Aziz was his real name; Aziz Jung was his title. He was an exceptionally brilliant administrator, and author of many books, of which covered many topics. He constructed Aziz Bagh for his personal residence.

Deen Yar Jung: Aliuddin Ahmed was his real name; Deen Yar Jung was his title. He was the third son of Aziz Jung. Like his father, he was also a man with many talents and administrative abilities.

Ghazi Yar Jung: Ghaziuddin Ahmed was his real name; Ghazi Yar Jung was his title. He was the first son of Aziz Jung. He was a very able high court judge.

Khan Bahadur: another title for Aziz Jung for his exceptional service.

Nawab: The kings called their noble men Nawab for their extraordinary services and administrative talents. Not to be confused with the Jagirdaars who were also referred to as Nawab. The Jagirdaars were randomly picked by the Kings to manage government properties for tax collection purposes only.

Shams-ul Ulema: Means 'Sun-Among-Scholars', another title given to Aziz Jung for his scholastic achievements.

Vila: Aziz Jung used this name when he wrote poetry.

Aziz-ul-Akhbar: Newspaper called 'Aziz-ul-Akhbar' was originally published by Nawab Aziz Jung from Aziz Bagh.

Tareeq-un-Nawayat: Nawab Aziz Jung traced his family lineage (Genealogy) all the way up to the Prophet Muhammed and called it 'Tareeq-un-Nawayat'.

52111969R00114

Made in the USA
Lexington, KY
11 September 2019